BEYOND THE PAIN

A RETURN TO LOVE

BEYOND THE PAIN

A RETURN TO LOVE

KEMI SOGUNLE

First printing, November 2016

LIBRARY OF CONGRESS CATALOGING-IN-PUBLICATION DATA.
ISBN: 978-0-9909721-4-3 (Print)
ISBN: 978-0-9909721-5-0 (eBook)

Cover Artwork designed by Freepik
Cover Design by Kemi Sogunle
Interior Layout by Maureen Cutajar

DISCLAIMER
Although the author has made every effort to ensure that the information in this book was correct at press time, the author does not assume and hereby disclaim any liability to any party for any loss, damage, or disruption caused by errors or omissions, whether such errors or omissions result from negligence, accident, or any other cause.

DEDICATION

This book is dedicated to my son, my gift from God...the love of my life, Tobi, who continues to bring the best out of me and allows me to deposit nuggets of love and wisdom daily in his life.

To my clients who allow me support them on their journey, I say thank you. To the readers who seek to know the truth that will set them free and return to love. To everyone who continues to support my purpose and help me become who God created me to be.

To God the Father, who continues to be my life, my strength, my all, my true love. The God the Son, for saving and rescuing me for the pit of hell. Thank You for the Cross that buried all my sins and shame, bringing love and light that no one can give. To God, the Holy Spirit, for guiding me and always nudging me in the right direction. Without the Trinity, I am nothing. Thank You, God for choosing this weak vessel and giving me wings to shine Your Light to the world. I stand in awe of You. To God be the Glory!

PREFACE

Every relationship you go through, leaves you with a life lesson. Life after all, is a teacher and can bring about blessings or pain depending on the outcome of each relationship as well as the choices you make. You will sometimes get hurt, become heartbroken, rejected or left with so much pain that may take a toll on you and result in a shift away from the course of your life's journey. However, you cannot remain defeated or continue to play a victim but you must find your way to heal, forgive and move on.

You may have tons of questions and wonder where to go from where you are. You may try to find reasons as to why you had to go through all the pain. Why did it have to be you? Why would someone who claims to love or have claimed to love you, leave you so devastated? Why do you feel broken and stuck with the pain?

Where do you start from? How do you heal and forgive? Is there life beyond the pain you are experiencing? Is there anything left for you to do? All these questions and more may flood your mind and you may start to feel depressed.

You however need to know that there is life beyond the hurt, the brokenness, the heartbreaks; rejection or fear. You must learn to unpack, unlearn and pull yourself back together again, for you to experience life *"Beyond the Pain and Return to Love."*

CONTENTS

INTRODUCTION

Pain can be acquired in so many ways and in such a short time. Pain never goes away...at least not all at once. We learn to peel off layers gradually, as we begin to heal. We tend to uncover more hidden pain as the layers start to come off.

Some of the issues, we had shoved underneath the rug and never thinking or hoping that they would resurface again. We only begin to sniff in the dust from such, when the truth starts to show up in our lives.

You suddenly realize that everything you were running away from has started to chase you down in ways you never expected. I remember having flashbacks during my healing process, after my painful divorce. I would get angry at myself and would sometimes cry and scream. I wanted the reality of what I thought was a dream to disappear but I had accumulated so much pain that everything began oozing from underneath the rug. It was like having a water line backup and flood the room. The padding under the carpet could no longer hold the water and it happens to be so soggy that both the carpet and the padding had to be thrown away. I had to stare at the blank floor. All the packaging was damaged and it was time to begin to peel back the layers of painful memories...from the moment I was raped at age 17, rejected by a boyfriend I thought was the one, to losing a friend who I confided in and how I had to face reality and deal with everything I thought would not come back to haunt me. I was determined to heal from everything...all those painful memories and experiences.

I realized I could not heal all at once. It will take several processes and stages. It took years to build those layers and it will take time to unpack and get rid of the emotional baggage. Like me, you may have gone through difficult seasons of life, had your heart broken by someone you loved, experienced divorce or lost a loved one but you cannot stay in that place of pain for too long. After all, no one deserves to live with pain. No one deserves to stay under. You and I must learn to let go of anything that no longer serve us. It is time to live the rest of our lives as the best years of our days on earth. We must learn to move beyond the pain and experience life again. It is time for the NEW YOU to emerge and evolve. It is time to allow yourself heal so that you can experience love again!

THE VERY BEGINNING...

TAKING A JAB AT LIFE!

No one provided any of us with life's manual. We all must learn to live and discover ourselves through all that we have been conditioned with based on culture, tradition and society. We try hard to navigate our ways through life, facing obstacles, scaling hurdles, getting bruised and burnt but fighting hard to strive and thrive. You may sometimes grow weary, pick up bad habits or take things out on your loved ones. Friends and family may not understand it and sometimes you may feel like everyone is after you. You may begin to stress out both personally and professional and can sometimes feel as if life should end. However, God continues to grant you breath so that you do not give up but realize that you have a journey and purpose you need to complete and fulfill.

You must be equipped to continue the path that lies in front of you while focusing on the present moment. You must see beyond the pain to become a better version of you while ensuring you live consciously and authentically. You must learn to trust the process, be patient and trust God even more than you have ever done. For me, it was looking at my journey and getting tired of repeating cycles and patterns.. No one can truly live and move forward without honestly dealing with the issues, healing from the painful past and becoming ready to move into purposeful living. I had to deal with the pain from being rape and face it. I had to dive into all the painful experiences and as I began to trace my steps back. I realized everything I had gone through was leading me to a better place...this only happened the moment I made the decision not to remain in denial but to face it all.

You may be reading this book and you are telling yourself that you do not need to reflect on buried issues but I want you to know that without addressing all the issues you have ignored, like 'karma,' they will creep in and steal your joy and peace..

I share my journey to healing in my book, *"Being Single: A State for the Fragile Heart."* I had to go through the soul searching and healing process which made me so sick to my gut that I could not believe some of the worst decisions I made without realizing the consequences, I had to face. Everything that I had gone through was now shaping me to become who God made me.

We sometimes do not know the depth of the choices we make in dire times. The consequences we face are so significant and can change or reshape us for the rest of our lives.

*What sometimes seemed to be minute
trials or temptation, suddenly become
enlarged in our own eyes that we
sometimes miss out on living yet,
God still grants us mercy and grace.*

We sometimes long for answers and wait for solutions but we are not patient enough to hear from God. We end up making quick and sometimes irrational decisions that break us. It may be getting in a relationship with the wrong partner, getting married for the wrong reasons, accepting a job offer not in line with God's plans (will) for us or starting a venture because everyone is doing it. That first jab however, may be the very one that derails or sidetracks us from the original Master Plan and will teach us all that we need to know to move into living truthfully and with purpose.

THE JOURNEY

As you read this book, I invite you to take this spiritual journey and learn how you can *"Move Beyond the Pain and Return to Love."* This journey will allow you see through the window of God's love and how everything that you have gone through or may be going through, will prepare you for the abundant life God designed for you from the very start. Going back to the basics is very necessary especially if you are ready to move from being stuck to becoming. For me, going back to the basics as a preacher's daughter was digging back into the Word of God. Although I grew up in the church: from singing in the choir to acting as part of the drama group and volunteering for different opportunities, finding myself was far from the radar. I did not know who I was then but I thought if I could fit in with everyone else, I would be okay. I was that shy (yet confident) little girl who did not want to participate in certain activities due to my upbringing.

We however, tend to learn more outside of our norm through interacting with others. After all, there is no manual or guide to life. You either begin by allowing others lead you to believe those things unsaid at home, that awaken your curiosity and make you believe that what you are now being told by others is the real deal. Your tentacles stand up and are loud to scream and embrace everything you have been told not to do. You want to begin to explore and as you become more and more inquisitive, you start to thirst for information that will help you break those walls built out of fear instilled in you as a child.

You finally found the key to unlock the mysteries of the unseen world that you have been shielded from taking a glance at. There is the adrenaline rush to get things going. You cannot wait to get your feet wet and learn about things you do not know nothing about. The temperature suddenly rises and viola, the door is opened for you to dive right in and get your share of the goodies. You can finally smell the freedom just like a teenager leaving home for college. You believe you no longer have to follow the rules. This is the beginning...the very beginning of adventure into life and living.

FROM BABY TO ADULTHOOD

You may not know who you are yet and finding yourself may be far from it. You are trying hard to figure out how everyone is getting ahead of the game but you are not yet there. As a baby, you were able to crawl around, cry and get the attention of your parents, siblings or family members. You got your diaper changed and you began seeking for attention when you see others getting into a comfortable state of conversation. No one stared at you or tried those baby cues to get your attention, so you had to learn how to scream or cry and everyone would suddenly become quiet. That was all you had to do the get the attention you needed. As you continue to grow older, you discover you can get into places without anyone stopping you.

You can climb through those "silly" gates they put up as barriers to stop you from getting hurt. You can crawl, walk and run. You have begun to gain your freedom from being carried around and strangers pulling your cheeks while calling you cute. Alas, you can run and hide at your own pace and have them chase after you. You are beginning to learn life skills that will go a long way but you are not quite there...it is still a very long way ahead. The attention may no longer be present and you are beginning to feel independent to some extent. Years go by quickly and you are off to kindergarten.

This is the beginning of a phase in your life that you may not have planned for but eventually must live and face. You may experience bullying from some of the children you get to interact with while in school and this may trigger some nerves in you such that you awaken fear and sometimes ego (as a form of self-defense). This may set the pace of some of the way you connect to negative energy and take the lessons learned turning them into good or bad habits and building on those skills (subconsciously or unconsciously).

The teenage year comes by and your level of curiosity constantly rises. The friendships you make, especially those that make you feel easily accepted, may expose you to the good or the bad. You will be introduced to habits and antics. You want to try out more things and your association with the wrong crowd suddenly begins to lead you into places of exploration and sometimes pain. You may never think about where it all started and the wrong relationships at the adolescent stages may continue to lead you into more of those types of places that weaken you and may later break you.

You may on the other hand, be fortunate enough to keep good company and none of these things apply to you. However, you still must face challenges and obstacles for trying to stand out and not fit in. This is the beginning of taking a jab at life. The very start of worrying and woes you never imagined. It may go on into college years and adulthood without you questioning the choices you are making and the consequences you are facing or may later face.

You get into relationships with others (friendship or romantic) and you experience so much disappointments, heartbreaks and pain. You may even experience divorce or death of a loved one and it all continues to weigh you down without ever taking a look at how it all begun. Are you beginning to see the picture? Are you now trying to put the pieces of the puzzle together? You may have to wait and learn not to rush the process. Rushing to analyze and dissect all the information in your bank will lead you to have regrets and may curse out but you do not need all that negative energy.

This book is written to help you connect the dots, the broken pieces you thought were no longer valuable. You will learn how everything fits together and realize why you did some of those things that you cannot even talk about.

PONDER ON THIS:

When did you begin to get curious about the things you had no knowledge about?

_____

_____

_____

_____

_____

_____

You may have been told that those things should never be of interest. Your culture or tradition may not buy into those things. It may be against family values but of interest to you. What do you do if this is the case?

_____

_____

_____

_____

_____

_____

Did You Know?

The very beginning...going back to the basics, was kicked off with God creating the earth and everything in it. He said, "Let there be light" and there was light.

Everything was good in God's eyes. He formed man after everything had been placed on earth but then, He noticed that Adam, the first man, was alone and needed someone of his type. Every creature God placed on earth came in pairs but man, Adam, had no one to pair up with. God decided to create Eve by putting

Adam to sleep. He instructed them and told them not to eat from the tree of knowledge of good and evil but the serpent showed up to awaken Eve's curious mind. His question to Eve was, "Did you know?"

Does that sound familiar? Do you recall someone awakening your curiosity by using those exact words? Hmm, can you recall when you suddenly gave in due to the same question? Has someone persuaded you to believe anything outside of your norm and were up for it? Did you somehow feel like an illiterate than needed to quick acquire the knowledge?

_____

_____

_____

_____

_____

_____

_____

You may not think of the consequences at that moment. All you wanted to do is acquire the knowledge but that may be the beginning of life's woes, your derailment from progress or your breakdown instead of a breakthrough. Eve was persuaded and deluded to believing that the fruit from the tree of knowledge of good and evil was all she needed to become enlightened. She gave in and quickly passed it on to Adam and both suddenly realized that they were naked. This is the same feeling you get when you discover something you never knew about. Think about the things you were exposed to (or may be exposed to, if you are a teenager reading this) and how that has led to some of the consequences you have had to face or may be facing at this present moment.

What was so enticing that you forget your needs, requirements or values? You may have given in to fit in. You got tired of standing out. You got fed up with being told that you cannot venture into those things. You took a leap and realized it tasted better on your tongue than you were told. The same story was told to Eve.

The deceiver said, "You will gain the knowledge and become like God." How curious could she have been? She wanted to become knowledgeable. She must have perceived and assumed lot of the possibilities that could result from her eating the fruit.

The beginning of curiosity should only lead to an awareness of who you truly are created to be.

You may wonder and fantasize but reality is that it will only end up in pain if it was not part of God's plan for you. You will become a stranger to your true essence.

This is the beginning of your journey into the world and away from the you God created you to be. I found myself yielding to the peer pressure of dating a guy as a teenager in high school. I attended a girls' only school but the boys always flocked to the entrance of the school after hours. The older girls seem to understand the game than some of us the younger ones. They shared stories and the romantic novels (Mills & Boon – I wonder if those are still in circulation, Sidney Sheldon's books, etc.) made it seems surreal. I had no clue of what to expect so I yielded to the pressure after all, we were about to graduate from high school. I could not think of any excuse to give them any longer but I would hear my mother's voice ringing in my ears not to allow any boy touch me. I was a bit reluctant at first but then I decided to talk to someone who had caught my eyes and was a friend to my brothers. I had also watched my brothers and their friends so I picked up some lessons from them.

Before this, I would have the boys flock to want to talk to me but I was not interested due to some of the pain I kept in from watching and listening to my parents argue. They had no idea that it emotionally affected me and I never talked about it. The truth is that we were not allowed to talk to our parents about certain things back then.

We were never caged in but the Christian principles that were imbibed in us, set the pace for my life. Tunde and I began talking and he protected me while always willing to listen and give advice when needed. High school was over and I would share some personal things with him (things I could not share with my brothers even though we were close...things about my parents and life in general). He always reassured me that everything was going to be okay and I gained a confidant. Tunde however, passed away during that summer...he drowned at a beach party and my world was shattered (you can read more from my book, *"Being Single: A State for the Fragile Heart"*).

I lost a friend who always protected me, never demanded for sex and was my listening ear and shoulder to cry on. I later buried my head in books and would sometimes cry myself to sleep. After a while, I summoned the courage to get back to normal even though I was still hurting inside. I allowed my friends to match-make and talk me into a relationship that led to my being raped at age 17. My curiosity to get back into reality, allowed friends persuade me about what I wanted (not what I needed) but would now end up in a consequence I had to face.

Eagerness can have its pros and cons but without thoroughly thinking and without weighing what the consequences could be, you can end up at the wrong place at the wrong time. I had the choice of turning down the birthday party invite. I ignored my intuition's call to action but wanted to have fun. I was shy in the midst of the crowd and very much an introvert but I had lost a friend and wanted to get back into normal. This was the beginning another level of pain that I did not deal with until I got divorced. The curiosity of dating and getting into the groove like everyone else, led me to give in to dating someone and yield to the peer pressure. I however, cannot blame them for my own choices. My choices were mine to own and deal with.

This is how we take a jab at life from the very beginning. We become curious, we want adventure, we want to learn something outside of our norm based on what others tell us or we observe that seem enticing and captivating. We give in and have to face the consequences. Eve must have looked at the fruit and saw how juicy it was. She was convinced that she would gain wisdom and be like God. She took a bite and handed it to Adam. They were both deceived. Do you see the pattern?

Can you relate to this? How easy is it to persuade you to believe something someone says or what you observe others doing?

_____

_____

_____

_____

_____

_____

It could be someone you admired (and still do) or have always wanted to be in a relationship with. Those words are way too captivating that you do not want to miss out on anything. You have to execute the game plan and give it a shot. Just like Adam and Eve, you and I fall into the same temptation or persuasion. We have no idea who God created us to be so we begin to seek for acceptance and answers.

You want to be accepted by friends who are trending or popular. You want to be where they are. You want that relationship so bad that you fall for empty words that will later result in your heart becoming broken. You felt he or she was the one for you but it ended up in divorce. Can you visualize how it all played out?

What did you believe at that point that you can pinpoint was never true but you persuaded yourself into?

_____

_____

_____

_____

_____

_____

How did it begin for Adam and Eve? The first couple God brought together and had it all. They were not facing any relationship issue. The garden had everything they needed. Before Eve arrived, Adam was formed in the image and likeness of God. God placed him in the garden to dominate and take care of everything He had created. Adam had a job. He worked the garden and was self-sufficient. He had a relationship with God and communed with Him regularly.

Adam however did not have someone of his kind to relate to and so God created Eve as a helpmate. This established the second type of relationship. The first is the relationship with God. The second is the relationship with Eve. God said whatever He put together, let no man put asunder. Eve was however alone for a moment when the serpent persuaded her to eat the fruit. Adam and Eve became one flesh.

There was no need or cause to doubt their existence or relationship. The introduction of a third party however, led to their separation from God's garden and peace. Their minds were undiluted (in alignment with God's will) before eating the fruit. An external and third party showed up and led them astray.

Do you see the similarities with your journey? How often do you allow someone come into your space and take your eyes off that which God has spoken about your life? How often do you invite third parties into your relationship and allow them contribute to what they did not put together? Do you allow your friends talk you into actions you know deep inside are not what you need or should be involved in?

_____

_____

_____

_____

_____

You may not have thought about it from this dimension but it is the reality of life.

CHALLENGE

What do you think will happen if you do not give in to persuasion?

_____

_____

_____

_____

_____

What lessons can you take away from this nugget?

_____

_____

_____

_____

_____

_____

What adjustments are you willing to make that will prevent you from facing tough consequences because of the choices you make?

_____

_____

_____

_____

_____

_____

What patterns were you able to identify? What actions are you going to take to stop you from repeating these patterns?

_____

_____

_____

_____

_____

_____

How are you going to align yourself with God's will and build on your relationship with Him?

_____

_____

_____

_____

_____

_____

WHY FALL FOR IT?

E ve was alone when the serpent approached her. There must have been a void that created a way for her to fall for the empty words. What could be going on in her mind at that moment? How excited could she be to discover that the fruit was going to make her like God. How enticing where the words uttered by the serpent?

Can you imagine what went through her mind?

The same applies to you and I in today's world. We become easily persuaded when we have a void and longing. It may be for a partner or to buy a product that we think will solve the problem to that longing and fill the void we have. Most of what is offered in that moment when there is that need outside of God's plan may however, be a temporary solution that you apply but still leaves you feeling empty or even emptier than the way it was before you bought it. This is because the temporary solution, which appears too good to be true, will only fulfill the want you had in that moment but will not satisfy your needs. It is like craving for ice-cream when thirsty but you really know what you need is water to quench your thirst.

You however buy the ice-cream and thirty minutes later; you begin to thirst again.

UNDERSTANDING THE CONNECTIONS

God created each one of us with a soul, mind and heart to be in unison. However, due to the culture, tradition and background we are raised in, we become conditioned and our composition becomes disconnected based on all we are made to believe and taught. We are originally created in God's image and after His likeness.

God created each one of us with a destiny aligned to a purpose and character He put together. Man however, tries to study you and tell you who you are outside of who God deemed you as.

> *Man cannot know the heart of God –*
> *His Will for each one of us is different.*

Man does not know the heart of God but tries to study you and I to tell us what is outside of God's plan. Hence, we become disillusioned to believing everything outside of God's plan and begin to run after man's plan, developing limited beliefs and begin to idolize each other or hate as one person begins to progress over the other. "The heart (of man) is deceitful above all things and beyond cure.

Who can understand it? I, the Lord, search the heart and examine the mind, to reward each person according to their conduct, according to what their deeds deserve" – Jeremiah 17: 9-10.

The moment the mind, which houses the thoughts, becomes disconnected from the soul and the heart (where the Spirit of God lives), we begin to wander away from God's plan for us. An altered state of mind or thoughts will only believe so many illusions that it creates either from heresies, poor choices made out of selfish reasoning, wrong advice or letting others dictate how you live and which direction you need to take. The truth is that when you are going through life, you have to obtain clarity by connecting to the Spirit of God within, the guide, comfort and source that God included in your being. The Spirit of God within connects us with God when we pray and seek His face for help.

God will always send someone to confirm what He has spoken to you when you are still unsure of what you heard from Him. Those people who God send are your purpose helpers who will help you stay on track so that you do not fall for the antics or gimmicks.

Before I became aware of the truth, I thought God put me through this terrible journey of life to make me suffer yet He says He loves me still. The moment I became aware of His love and compassion, I made up my mind NEVER to allow anyone make me shift or drift away from it. Most of the time, we are not able to see the truth because we are clouded by the persuasion and manipulation of others.

How did Eve fall for the serpent's persuasion? It began with the question, "Did you know that if you eat of this tree, this fruit, you will become...?"

PONDER ON THIS:

How often times do you get persuaded to believing something based on a question asked? How often do you think that person may have studied you to find out where you are in your journey and so has set out to derail you by bringing you a temporary solution to soothe the longing you have at that very moment but may not be the solution you need for a lifetime?

_____
_____
_____
_____
_____
_____

How long did it take you to realize that the need was never met but the temporary solution massaged your pain for a short period?

_____
_____
_____
_____
_____
_____

The soul and mind become disconnected from the heart, where the Holy Spirit lives, leading to chaos and illusions within the thought process. Hence, you begin to wander off track and can no longer connect to God's plan at that point. Deviating from God's plan stops you from 'becoming' and 'evolving' into the real you He created, loved and equipped to be WHOLE. What have you believed outside of God's plan that has led you far from your truth?

_____

_____

_____

_____

_____

_____

THE SOUL, HEART AND MIND

The soul, heart and mind all live in the body. A disconnection from one can lead to a breakdown of the others. The breakdown can further lead to a disconnection that will prevent you from hearing God speak to you through the Holy Spirit in your times of need. It is however, essential to know how to keep the three areas intact...connected and in sync.

The soul is where all the longing and yearning take place. The soul longs for a connection with God but due to all the distractions in the world you live in, it begins to search for worldly pleasures while allowing your emotions play a part in leading you in the opposite direction...away from God. Thoughts occur in the mind and often times, when you are in pain or feel broken, you cannot reason positively or hear God speak to your heart. The human thought process becomes disillusioned as your emotions begin to become awakened and create scenarios (assumptions) and speculate all sorts of actions that are born out of imagination and fantasies. This is also where the lust of the flesh begins...wandering away of man's soul from God's plan and will.

Adam and Eve never knew they were naked until the serpent showed up. Eve's mind was lost in her thoughts of finding a temporary and quick solution to gain understanding hence, she fell for it and at the fruit after so much persuasion.

> *It is easy to be persuaded, manipulated and deceived into believing something when you have been alone for a while and long to have someone in your life.*

Your emotions are awakened at that point with so much chaotic thoughts of what will look or feel like for you. However, the disconnection between the heart, mind and soul, prevents you from hearing God's guidance and words for the next steps you need to take. Someone suddenly shows up and you give in to the empty words without actions after the sweet and deceptive words have exhibited a connection with where you are emotionally. Alas, you find yourself in cloud nine and man-made imaginary fantasy world. The serpent has found its way to you in your lonely moment and will manipulate and deceive you while appearing to look like the real deal.

Can you recall any event that occurred in the past, where you gave in to deceptive words and manipulation due to your emotional state of mind and loneliness? How did the decisions you made back then affected your journey to this date?

_____

_____

_____

_____

_____

_____

THE CONDITIONED MIND

You and I were born into the sinful world and became conditioned from birth.

Conditioned with the words spoken to us, the things we learned and continue to learn from others as well as what we observe…the happenings around us. The conditioned mind gradually becomes disconnected from the spiritual being that you are, your true essence. The conditioned mind is led to believe everything outside of God's plan and begins to become consumed with limited beliefs.

Beliefs that may have been imbibed in you from birth, thus restricting you to learn anything outside of that realm and prevent you from figuring out who you are. These beliefs limit your perspective and hold you in a space of bondage. This is one of the reasons we face so much problems in the world today. Allowing man established culture and tradition to hold you captive from seeing the way God originally designed it to be.

The truth however, is that it is hard to de-condition the human mind but without doing it, you will not be able to release yourself from the pain or past and allow God to open your eyes and help you understand His plans for you. Without freeing yourself from this state, you will allow the culture and tradition to hold you captive from seeing through God's eyes and limit your vision to that of man which is already misguided. The conditioned mind is led to live in fear and create illusions within the thoughts which then create a false mindset and prevent you from the reality but makes you put up a façade. You will only be able to see what you want everyone else to believe or what you have been conditioned to believe.

You may ask, "How is it that the mind is conditioned?" Right from birth, you may have been fed with fears by your parents, siblings, friend or family members.

This leads you to staying away from certain things...food, people or environment.

You cannot trust others based on your conditioned mind. You find yourself analyzing everything based on your limited beliefs. You are made to believe that some of the things you go through are based on God's plans, forgetting that your choices and actions will result in the consequences you face. You are made to become insecure to some extent and your judgement and reasoning become clouded and limited.

Every thought gives birth to illusions or positive reasoning but it is up to you to determine how you process your thoughts towards positive or negative choices that cause you to obtain the results and consequences you will or are facing.

Your inquisitive mind also contributes to your decisions which may be based on the conditioning of your mind which prevent you from thinking outside the realm you know. It is so easy to have your mind become conditioned when you are persuaded to believe empty words with no actions or buy into an idea that may not be part of God's plan for you. Eve became conditioned the moment the serpent fed her with lies. She was already vulnerable and he took advantage of the fact. She allowed herself to become manipulated and this led to separation from God's plan.

Every thought happens in the mind and this is one of the reasons why God said, "His thoughts are not our thoughts neither His ways our ways." ~ Isaiah 55: 8

Can you relate to this? How have you become conditioned by your upbringing...culture, tradition, beliefs? How have these affected your reasoning and decision making?

_____

_____

_____

_____

_____

_____

YOUR THOUGHTS

Thoughts are the most dangerous culprits in the mind of humans. You wrestle with positive and negative thoughts, struggling to make the decisions that can lead to a breakdown and result in a drastic diversion from your true course in life. You may be going through a difficult situation and find it hard to hold on to the positive thoughts. Decisions made during difficult times can change your life for the better or for the worse.

This is the reason God provided us with the Holy Spirit to teach, comfort and guide us in all our ways while helping us align our minds and thoughts with the will of God. Jesus Christ taught the disciples how to pray and laid a blueprint for us to follow so that when we are lonely or in need, we can come to the Father through the Holy Spirit, to obtain clarity. Hence, we are reminded in 1 Corinthians 2: 11, "For who knows a person's thoughts except their own spirit within them? In the same way, no one knows the thoughts of God except the Spirit of God."

Without connecting to the Spirit of God within, you cannot align your thoughts with God's and you will only be left to tinker on what you have being conditioned with by humans. Thoughts outside of God's vision for your life, will lead to a shift away from the things of God and towards the flesh, illusions will be created out of fear, worry and anxiety. Your life can also be affected by the thoughts of those you choose to surround yourself with. If you find yourself surrounded by those hurting, all you will acquire and offer is the pain you have experienced and they are experiencing.

You will exist in a place of pain. Your conversations will make you become angry, worried or resentful. Your thought process will only be around those things that hold in you the painful space. You will carry negative energy and will barely hold on to anything positive. You will find yourself more emotionally destabilized and mentally drained thus affecting your wellbeing and health. You may find yourself pretending to be happy in the presence of others but breaking down when alone. At this point, you are far away from who you truly are. Your thoughts will now define who you think you are.

Have you found yourself getting angry and unable to control your thoughts? Have you taken the time to think about the choices that you made that may have resulted in the consequences you are facing or have faced? What was the outcome of your evaluation of the situation? What can you deduce from such experiences?

_____

_____

_____

_____

_____

_____

YOUR EMOTIONS

God provided you and I with emotions so that we do not get far away from Him but draw closer to Him when we become overwhelmed or face challenges.

We can go to Him to obtain the grace and strength we need to go on living. However, due to the mind becoming conditioned, we have been taught and have learned to channel our emotions toward anger, malice, resentment, bitterness, revenge or judgement. You become disconnected from the source and the most important relationship that was established...your relationship with God. This severance leads to seeking others for validation, approval and acceptance. The longing for approval, acceptance or validation usually results in you getting hurt by others than finding the answers to the situation. Instead, you discover that problems continue to rise as well as conflicts.

Without knowing where to turn in times of conflict or turmoil, you will turn to others and forget God, the solid foundation of your being and creation. Your soul will continue to yearn and long for solutions to fill the void in your life. You find yourself acting out towards others, settling for a relationship you will never want to get into and thinking irrationally yet unable to make wise decisions. You crave for attention, affection and validation and may fall into the hands of deceivers, manipulators and fail to connect your mind, soul and heart in unison to hear from God.

Those irrational decisions coupled with illusions, imagination and fantasy, may make you believe that others have a part to play in your predicaments. Reality however, is that every time you are having an emotional roller coaster ride, you are reminded of areas where you need to work on in your life...areas of weaknesses that you need to turn into strengths. This is a spiritual awakening to connect to your conscious and true self with the opportunity to grow and become stronger while learning the lessons that stage of your life brings.

How will you channel your emotions towards your growth? How can you recognize the emotional waves when they show up?

_____

_____

_____

_____

_____

_____

Whenever you get angry or emotional, the opportunity arises for you to connect to God and reason with Him. It is a spiritual awakening to reality and away from the conditioning, façade or denial. The emotions you allow to dominate your present moments will determine what becomes your reality.

You have the right to choose what you can do in that moment. You can choose to be angry, resentful, bitter but you have to remember that anger is a choice, bitterness is a choice, keeping malice is a choice so is resentment and without becoming conscious of who you truly are through spiritual awakening of my mind, you will continue to connect emotionally to who you are not.

> *Bitterness is a choice. Forgiveness is a choice. Freedom is a choice. Love is a choice. Healing is a choice. Whatever you choose, becomes your reality. Choose wisely!*

I became aware of this stage of my life during my healing process. I realized how I allowed all the illusions and conditioning from birth into adulthood, limited my beliefs and held me back from aligning myself with my spirituality and connect to The Creator, God. As I continued to study the word of God, I realized that God rarely got angry. Whenever He did as it was documented in the bible, destruction occurred to wipe away corruption, evil and sinful acts of men. He got angry when Adam and Eve disobeyed His commands. He showed anger towards the people of Israel in the days of Noah, wiping out the earth except for Noah and his family. He did the same with Pharaoh and his men, allowing them to become buried beneath the Red Sea. God is emotionally stable and as long as we are created in His image and after His likeness, our emotional DNA should match up.

Your emotions are brought to the surface when the mind, heart and soul are disconnected.

You may find it difficult processing the truth and can become emotionally manipulative and controlling. Your ego is awakened and fear becomes part of the picture. You may become numb to your truth as a result of this. You may begin to find solutions in the wrong places while trying to justify the reasons why you are taking the steps you towards negative behaviors. Anyone who does not agree with you suddenly becomes an enemy. Due to emotional instability, your self-esteem may become lowered and insecurities escalate. Past painful experiences that may have led to rejection, abuse or brokenness may limit your beliefs and allow you to defend yourself with ego while trying to hide behind your emotions.

Without seeking for help to get out of this state, you will experience more pain, hurt, rejection and most of these will be self-inflicted.

Connecting to your intuition...the Spirit of God within, can help you shift from an unstable emotional state, overcome fear, get rid of anger, bitterness and fear and lead you to becoming humble and subduing ego. You must "... guard your heart for therein flows the issues of life (Proverbs 4: 23)." Guarding your heart allows you to control your emotions and thoughts, turn your negative energy into a positive one, when you connect with God and receive His love. Association with love results in meaningful conversations, peaceful communication and relationship with results.

You cannot operate from a place of love when you are emotionally unstable. You cannot receive the people God sends to you as your purpose helpers when you are experiencing an emotional roller coaster ride and ego is awakened. Your emotions should bring you to the awareness of your true essence and trigger something positive within you that will lead you to prayerfully connect with God to obtain clarity.

Pain awakened due to emotions will only rob you of truthful living and the life God designed for you. Emotionally holding on to painful experiences will only cloud your judgement and decision making leaving you to become bitter not better.

You become numb to the truth and hold on to the lies you may be telling yourself or others may tell you. You end up finding yourself becoming comfortable to settle and be around those who will not bring the truth to your awareness.

WOMEN AND EMOTIONS

As a woman, your emotions allow you to connect and relate to others in different ways. God created you as a helpmate to support your partner's vision and help him become a better man. This is the same way God draws your attention back to Him when you are stuck or may be on the wrong path. A woman who is spiritually grounded and connected with God, will draw the attract those who are spiritually grounded and connected to God. If there is any area of your life that needs to grow, you will attract people who are operating on that level. However, if you are disconnected...your soul, mind and heart are not in sync, you are liable to run on emotions especially when lonely. This will bring men who will test you and bring to your attention, those deficit areas where you need to grow and become better.

You may find yourself analyzing and persuading yourself at this stage that a man showing up must mean you are ready especially if you are feeling lonely. You however, have to remember that as the stronger vessel, you cannot allow your emotions to lead you into the wrong places.

You are a temple and priced jewel but if you are not in sync with your soul, mind and heart, you will run with your emotions and your head, forgetting who you are, forgetting your requirements and you settle only to get hurt at the end of the day.

As a married woman, you have to ensure your vision and that of your husband are aligned. God gave Adam a vision and Eve was created out of him to help him fulfill the vision. You are emotionally and spiritually connected and have the motherly instincts to support your partner with birthing that vision to life. You are able to stand in the gap and pray as God reveals those areas to you. However, if you are not in sync with your mind, soul and heart spiritually, you will find faults and your tone of communication will not allow your partner to receive what God is showing you in that moment. You are able to connect to the revelation when all three areas of your life are in sync and can effectively communicate the message to your partner in love so that he can receive it. You have to remember that men are generally egoistical and process things logically and differently from the way women do.

Noah's wife was a woman who was not talked about in the bible. God gave Noah a vision to build an ark but she was supportive without raising a fight or creating drama. She recognized the vision and stood by and with him through the process (Genesis 6-8). There was no documentation of her forcefully or emotionally challenging him. Another reason why women are emotionally stronger is their ability to give birth. As a mother, you are able to recognize a child's cry and know when something is not right. This is a spiritual part of a woman's emotions that she may not realize. God sees our needs before we realize we have a need and steps into provision just as a mother does with a child.

This is one of the reasons a woman must be connected to her core...soul, mind and heart...connecting to God to be able to see the direction God is leading her.

As a woman you also have to realize that you were created out of a man and should never allow your emotions to lead you to the wrong man. Your heart (the home of the Spirit of God within you), should guide your thoughts, (your mind) and soul (where you experience the longing and yearning of a companion when lonely). Without this connection, you will allow your soul and mind lead you to settle and emotionally pour out into the wrong partner who may lead you to feel overwhelmed without reciprocating the affection you are giving to him. You will become emotionally drained, overwhelmed and depleted thus beginning to get angry and become hurt. Without that solid foundation and connection to your spirituality, you may be running on emotions that lead to nowhere.

> *Your gift from God is to be a helpmate that will support your partner with birthing his God-given vision for your union to life. Your effort however, will be futile when you are not in sync with your true essence (spirit, soul and mind).*

How have your emotions affected your relationship with yourself, your partner or husband? How has your relationship affected your relationship with others?

_____

_____

_____

_____

_____

_____

What actions or steps are you planning to make going forward that will allow you connect more with your true being that with your emotions?

_____

_____

_____

_____

_____

_____

MEN AND EMOTIONS

Men are more logical thinkers and always weigh out all their options before allowing others to see their emotional side. Thinking that a man is not emotional is a myth. Men do not often show their emotions because they do not want to be perceived as a weak vessel. Men internalize a lot and you may never know what a man is going through. A man usually has a preconceived idea and maps out a strategy to execute a plan with the hope that it will go well.

A man's emotions coupled with his thoughts and preconception which may lead to him become fearful, awaken ego. This is one of the reasons why men tend to put up a front and package themselves when trying to woo a woman. A man who is not aware of his true essence or who has been hurt but has not taken the time to heal, will struggle with his thoughts, longing and connection to his heart.

Every premeditated plan happens in his head. This unconscious and subconscious state of mind, leads him to create illusions and fantasize. A man who is broken, rejected or has experienced childhood pain and has not taken the time to heal with at this point, create fantasies and illusions due to the pain he carries in his mind, that will lead him to make irrational decisions that create a 'player' out of his pain.

If he connects with a woman who has healed and who brings to his awareness areas where he needs to work on and grow, he will cling to his ego as a form of self-defense and become upset with her. His pain and emotions lead him to want to control a relationship...he does not want to face defeat, heartbreak or pain anymore but connecting to the negative emotions at this stage prevents him from facing reality and connecting with his true self.

A man who is spiritually alert and conscious of himself (his being) will be able to relate to a woman who speaks life to him and sit to process what was said thoughtfully with positive reasoning without allowing his emotions to interfere with the process. He is able to connect to love and make amends where needed.

He may not allow the woman see him in that moment, but will later acknowledge your contributions towards his growth by showing appreciation.

A man may have good intentions but allow his emotional instability lead him astray when it comes to decision making especially when he is operating in pain. Men who have not taken the time to heal, feel insecure and are emotionally unavailable or unstable, use sex as a soother of their pain. Giving yourself as a woman, to such a man will allow you accumulate more emotional pain and tie your soul to him through sex.

This further leads you to become even more disconnected from your true essence (*I addressed the issue of soul ties in my book, "Being Single: A State for the Fragile Heart."*)

Truth: You must become aware of your emotional state and not allow your emotions lead you to become angry, resentful, to self-loathe and depression. Do not allow your emotions lead to you settling for less than you deserve. You must find the strength from within by choosing to connect to the Spirit of God within you when lonely or feeling hurt...draw from His well and receive grace to get back up.

Emotions will prevent you from receiving love when it shows up while you are hurting. God always sends love our way in times of pain, hurt or need. Love shows up to correct you but if you are running on emotions, you will see it as judgement. *"Better is open rebuke than hidden love. Wounds from a friend can be trusted but an enemy multiplies kisses" – Proverbs 6: 5-6.* Your willingness to accept the truth even though it hurts allows you to move into a space of peace, love and grace.

Your emotions are not intended to lead you to hurt others but without gaining consciousness of who you truly are created to be, you will continue to run high on emotions and remain disconnected from your true being and essence.

PONDER ON THIS:

Can you identify ways in which you allowed your emotions to prevent you from receiving love or from growing to a higher self? What did you learn from the situation? How can you prevent it from happening again?

_____

_____

_____

_____

_____

What do you plan on doing differently from now on with the awareness you have gained about emotions?

_____

_____

_____

_____

_____

_____

What goals do you plan to set that will help you with this and what timeframe will you set to meet these goals?

_____

_____

_____

_____

_____

_____

KNOWING THE DIFFERENCE
BETWEEN LOVE AND FEAR

Fear and love exist in the physical, mental and spiritual realms. Love however, operates on the spiritual level where your true essence lives. You have to understand that you are a spiritual being and you live in a physical body. You were created by God with love and born with love...love is part of your DNA and can never be removed from your composition. As you evolve and emerge, you become less fearful and more loving. However, knowing the difference between fear and love is vital to your growth and journey in life.

> *The closer you are to God (building your relationship deeper and deeper daily), the better and easier it will be for you to connect with love and eliminate fear.*

Fear holds you bound through the connection with illusions and thoughts in your mind. It makes you play and believe you are a victim of circumstances and can leave you feeling angry, resentful and revengeful. Choosing to remain in fear however, awakens ego as a form of self-defense mechanism to protect yourself. All fearful events happen in the physical realm. You may find yourself struggling to get out of it but because of the hurt you may have incurred and may be holding on to, you find it difficult to move from the physical level of pain to a spiritual level of healing and love. *"For we wrestle not against flesh and blood, but against principalities, against powers, against the rulers of this dark world and against spiritual wickedness in high places" – Ephesians 6: 12.*

Everything you wrestle with in your thought process, lives in the flesh (your mind and soul), not in your spirit. The powers of darkness that lie within your thoughts and everything that is outside of God's plan for you, holds on to fear and ego. Choosing to stay in the painful state however, will prevent you from making a shift towards evolving into the you God created from the inception. Your flesh wants to stay carnal but your heart and spirit want to bring you to the presence of God...rebirth into your divine purpose.

The ability to reason, learn and accept whatever happened in the past to gain wisdom, leads you into the conscious space of connecting to your spiritual being...the you born to fulfill your purpose. The moment you connect to this space and allow yourself to experience God's unconditional love, you begin to see yourself in a different light and understand what it means to love yourself before loving others. Once you have learned to love yourself completely, you can give and show the love that you are made of to others without hurting anyone. You will fully understand that, *"There is no fear in love but perfect love drives out fear, because fear has to do with punishment"* – 1 John 4: 18.

Fear led you to experience self-inflicted pain due to the illusions and worry you held on to in your thought process. You did not have to go through all of it but you were not aware of the depth of God's love for you.

Adam and Eve had to go into hiding after their eyes became opened due to fear. They were afraid of the consequences of their actions but eventually had to be punished for it. Fear will lead you to become resentful, anger, bitter...to live in hurt or pain due to the shame of your actions. Fear awakens ego and makes you remain silent hence breeding hurt, anger, malice, strife, resentment and bitterness.

You cannot operate from a place of love when fear, hurt, bitterness, resentment and anger are present in your life. You will only breed violence, the fruit of fear.

Where true love exists, fear, resentment, anger, gossip and hurt or pain cannot thrive.

Fear is associated with sin and sin with punishment. To live in fear is to hold yourself in a place of secrecy, shame and violence. Your thoughts go to war within you, your soul becomes restless and you are disconnected from your spirit where truth lies. You find yourself constantly making up lies to cover up for fear and shame. The more lies you tell, the further away you are from the truth. You cannot envision the truth and will not be able to comprehend it when someone brings it to your attention. You will fight whoever it is and begin to see them as your enemy because you have allowed fear to dominate and take over your mind and thoughts. You have awakened ego as a form of self-defense to stay within the realm of self-inflicted punishment that God never created. You cannot reason with the Spirit of God within you and most of the time, the prayers uttered in this state are out of fear and not pure.

Fear will only keep you in a place of suffering if you do not overcome it. Remember, it is born out of all your illusions and thoughts based on shame and sin. It is not real, can and will torture you until you learn to embrace the truth. It will make you become toxic to yourself while thinking others are against you.

CONQUERING FEAR

To begin conquering fear, you have to face the fear you have created from illusions, fantasies, negative emotions and thoughts as well as limited beliefs and pain that you may carry from childhood. You cannot avoid dealing with these areas if you want to move forward. Fear is usually created after a painful experience or information deposited during your journey in life. Fear punishes your soul and afflicts your health (body). Your spirit will always be alive but due to the disconnection, you may not be able to see beyond the pain. Fear is an illusion that is created within the thought process. Fear is not real but tries to make you believe that you can avoid dealing with the pain you have experience and create a perfect world that does not really exist.

Fear will allow you to set unrealistic expectations that lead to more pain and worry when they are not met. You will be left disappointed and repeat patterns. The more you gain awareness of who you are in God, the more you realize that fear does not exist. *"The Lord is my light and my salvation; whom shall I fear? The Lord is the strength of my life, of whom shall I be afraid?"* – Psalm 27: 1. You have to be determined, prepared and ready to change your mindset if you want to conquer fear. Your words have to match up with your actions. You have to constantly affirm yourself and take gradual steps as you profess and work towards the change.

You have to learn to forgive yourself for not knowing what you know now back then. You have to forgive those who hurt you and make restitution. You have to show yourself kindness, speak the truth even when a part of you wants to avoid facing reality and love yourself deeply. You will need to close the gap that exists between you and those who hurt you and awakened fear in you by reaching out to them and extending the grace of God you have received to them in love while letting them know you forgive them and set yourself free from the bond of hurt and pain that exist between you. You may have to write a letter if you do not want to see them face to face.

CHALLENGE

Take some time out to reach out to those who have hurt you or caused you pain in the past and extend forgiveness to them. Write down what you experienced as you spoke with them or wrote them. Notice the burden that was lifted from your mind and thoughts. If you wrote a letter, how did reading the letter make you feel? If you got a response back, what did it feel like reading from them? If you held a conversation, how did it go and what did you notice? What did you learn from this exercise (note: this challenge is to help you uncover hidden pain and learn to let go)?

_____

_____

_____

_____

_____

_____

DEALING WITH ANGER

Anger like fear, resides in the physical and mental realm of your being. You choose to connect to anger when you allow your thoughts control you rather than you controlling your thoughts. You get angry because things did not go your way and your plans were not executed...your expectations were not met. This is all part of self-will. Self-will allows you to seek after things or situations that will be beneficial to you alone without thinking of what others can gain from it or how you can be of influence to someone else. This is living outside of the spiritual realm where positive reasoning takes place. You are not able to reason positively because you are disconnected from God and connected to the world. You must realize that things will not always go your way especially if you are looking to satisfy your temporary wants and pleasures than fulfill a purpose God created you for.

Everything outside of God's plans will fail you in a matter of time and when you least expect it.

The moment you find yourself getting angry, ask yourself, *"What is leading me to become angry?" "Is there any lesson in this situation that I need to learn?" "Is there something about me that needs to change and grow?" "Is there truth in what is being said to me?"* Remember, love and anger cannot live in the same space. Love respects and speaks the truth always (even though it may seem hurtful when your ego is alive). Learn not to respond when truth is being spoken but take the time to reflect on what you heard and let it sit with you for a moment as you process the thoughts. Getting angry will not lead to your growth or maturity. Truth however, results in a spiritual awakening that invites you into a space of love and freedom from painful past and into conscious and truthful living.

PONDER ON THIS:

Every time you get angry, write down what you heard and what you believe triggered you to become angry. What did you learn?

_____

_____

_____

_____

_____

_____

What was the hidden gem in the message that held the truth leading you to become angry?

_____

_____

_____

_____

_____

_____

Did your conversation open up a wound you had showed under the rug? Were you able to view the situation from a different perspective and not from a place of pain? What did you realize when you did?

_____

_____

_____

_____

_____

_____

Dealing with Desires and Ego

Ego often times will tell you to revenge and awakens the desire to go all out and hurt more people because you have been hurt by someone. This takes place in your subconscious or unconscious state of mind...the physical and mental realms.

The main cause is brokenness. You have been hurt over and over and it has built up layers of pain that you may have become numb to. You are not consciously aware that you need to heal from this or may not know how to heal or what to do to move on. Hence, ego dominates and says, *"I refuse to be defeated. I refuse to be let down. I will dominate, be in control of everything from now on and go out living my life without addressing the pain."*

The moment you awaken ego, you wake up pride and open your mind to negative thoughts that will make you believe the lies that emerge from irrational thinking and illusions. This allows you to create deceptive schemes that lead you to manipulating and controlling others. Underneath this, your spirit within your heart seeks to connect with your mind and soul to help you seek and receive true love that you need but because of the pain you are carrying, your soul yearns for answers and your mind rages with illusions from the pain, leaving you to struggle within yourself...awakening a battle of the mind, spirit and soul.

The truth which your spirit wants to reveal cannot be received because of the state of your mind at this moment. This may lead you to suffer unconscious identity crisis.

You may find yourself trying to present the real you to others but the hurtful you shows up and dominates. This drives you to become angrier when those you are trying to hurt bring the truth to light.

Continuing on this path awakens the alter ego you create from the struggles you are experiencing...your spirit wants to be free but your mind and soul are held in bondage of pain. It is at this stage that the player in you emerges and awakens the sexual side of you. You may desire to have a good partner but wrestling with your thoughts and pain, cannot seem to allow your true intentions become known and your ego deprives you of living but you exist and defend your actions that do not match up with your words. You are also not able to accept corrections at this stage as you deem correction judgement of your hurt and pain.

Understanding Ego

Ego is usually awakened by emotional pain. It is a form of self-defense mechanism to shut off pain and to awaken fear and insecurities. Fear appears before ego shows up while ego follows suit when you come across someone who reminds you of the pain or hurt you had previously experienced. Every time you experience a flashback, ego shows up to defend you and brings along fear.

Defense is a form of make believe, that you are protected from repeating patterns. However, when you remember the incident, your mind wants to go out to hurt another man or woman who reminds you of the person who originally hurt you. You found out that the other people you hurt have a facial resemblance to the person who hurt you. A part of you still loves them hence you find yourself attract to someone who exhibits the same character. You begin to get close and as they try to show you love, ego shows up to defend you from receiving the love, reminds you of the pain and establishes the revenge mechanism.

Ego aka pride, takes you further away from God without you knowing. You become disconnected from your spiritual being and your focus is more on the physical and fleshy side of you. Psalm 10: 4 paints the picture of someone who is ego-centric, *"In his pride the wicked man does not seek Him (God); in all his thoughts there is no room for God."* Ego makes you become resentful and can only think of attacking others than loving them. Proverbs 13: 10, *"Where there is strife, there is pride, but wisdom is found in those who take advice."* Ego prevents you from receiving the truth and can lead you to become a player seeking to hurt others unconsciously or subconsciously.

As discussed in my book, *"Love, Sex, Lies and Reality,"* players do not wake up to want to become one neither do cheaters. They have gone through deep cut wounds that have not healed but because something triggers the memory to connect with the painful experiences, ego becomes awakened with fear and they go out to hurt new partners in the process. They shut off any form of communication so that words cannot be communicated that will bring back the pain. This exposes their insecurities to others. If you have been hurt by such a person, know that it was not intentional but because they exist in the subconscious and unconscious state and they are working hard to numb the pain rather than heal from it, they end up in a power struggle that pushes them out to hurt others. It is vital that you take the time to heal and become free so that you can connect to your spirituality, allow your mind and soul to be in sync with your heart and receive love from within to become free.

Your soul finds ego in fear. Your mind finds ache in pain but your heart finds love when free.

EGO AND YOUR RELATIONSHIP

Relationships experience ups and downs and can sometimes lead to breakups, heartaches and if ego is awakened during the relationship, it will only destroy it.

If you take a deep look at relationships across the globe, ego shows up whenever there is a conflict in our personas. No one wants to accept defeat due to fear of failure and as long as we do not recognize that fear has no place in love, we will continue to face challenges in our relationships. The world would be at peace if individuals will let go of ego, realize that love covers a multitude of wrongs and become humble while resolving issues by taking turns to listen to one another and reason before reacting. Love always heals but you cannot heal until you gain the understanding that you were created in love and you are love. Each one of us is born with love and God, who is love Himself, created us with love. Ego however, comes to play to distort this reality. This is why there is the struggle with flesh and blood. You and I are spiritual beings and the physical aspect of who we are is at constant war. The physical being invites ego and focuses on the external than the internal where the spirit lives.

You have to learn to stay mentally strong, aligning your mind, soul and heart in unity with God's will, realizing that love is stronger than pride and healing has to take place for you to operate in love. Ego blocks your ability to see the blessings your partner brings into your relationship when you hold on to pain. Becoming more spiritually awakened, enlightens the dark areas where pain is and allows you to overcome the power struggle. As you submit to God in humility, you ask Him to strengthen and heal you from within so that you can thrive. This will allow you learn from your partner, listen more to him or her and share the love you both have without holding on to grudges or pain. With love comes life and light, effective communication and you are able to build into one another so that you can become stronger, wiser and better together.

A life of humility has no pride or ego but love. Learn to let go of ego and hold on tightly to love. Love conquers all and covers a multitude of wrongs.

How has ego prevented you from receiving the truth in the past?

_____

_____

_____

_____

_____

_____

What do you plan on doing to recognize love when it shows up without awakening your ego?

_____

_____

_____

_____

_____

_____

The Relationships

Know that you are becoming aware of your true self, it is important to know and identify the role of people who come into your life. God handed you the script but you have to know who plays important roles. Not everyone you meet is looking out for you or wants your progress and success. Without understanding who you are, you open yourself up to everyone without setting boundaries or defining your requirements, establishing your goals and standards. Do not get me wrong, there are people you will meet to render help to but not allow into your space to know all your business. Remember that your life is a journey that comes with a purpose for you to fulfill. Allowing everyone in will derail you from the purpose and contribute to your painful experiences.

IDENTIFY INDIVIDUAL ROLES

Everyone you meet has a role to play in your life's journey but it is essential that you know who is who. Discerning who they are and what part the play by seeking God's face, will prevent you from allowing people into areas where they have not part in.

> *People come into your life to teach, break, shape and awaken you to growth.*

This applies to knowing who is a potential partner who is your 'rib' from those who come to play and waste your time. Without knowing who is who, you will get hurt, become upset and angry and created unnecessary drama and enemies while holding on to grudges and self-inflicting pain.

As you move along in life, you have to surround yourself with those who are able to sharpen you and help you become the best version of yourself. Those who bring to your awareness, the missing pieces of the puzzle that will help you connect to your God-given purpose. Without these people, you will find yourself surrounded by those who want you to remain where they are and not become better but bitter. In my book, *"Being Single: A State for the Fragile Heart,"* I discussed knowing who your purpose helpers, purpose pushers and purpose stoppers are. Your purpose helpers are those God send to help you connect and remain in your purpose, especially if you begin to fall astray. Your purpose pushers ensure you do not stay in your comfort zone. They may sometimes come in form of those who hurt you and lead you to grow. You do not see them as a problem but they allow you to focus on the solutions you need to continue on your journey.

The purpose stoppers are there to derail you and ensure you do not continue with God's purpose. They try to draw you back into the things of the flesh than allow you to connect to the gift of the spirit. They come with drama of all sorts and if you are not strong enough, you fall for their antics and right into the sinful nature.

Joseph met several purpose stoppers on his journey. Joseph was sold to slavery by his brothers, who were indirectly his purpose pushers. He ended up in Potiphar's house where he was second in command. Potiphar's wife however tried to seduce him but he escaped. She held on to his cloak and claimed that he was attempting to sleep with her. Joseph was able to escape because he was consciously aware of who and whose he was and knew what is God-given purpose was. He was however thrown in jail where he met some of his purpose helpers. He had interpreted their dreams and when they got out of jail, they forgot about Joseph. It was not the ripe timing for Joseph to get out of jail but when the time arrived, the cupbearer introduced Joseph to the king and God used him (Joseph) to prepare the Israelites for the great famine and save them from starving. Joseph was elevated and stepped right into his purpose.

You have to seek God's face to find out everyone's purpose when you meet each individual. You also have to remember you are here on earth for a purpose. Your focus should not be so much about the other people but about how they are connected to your purpose.

PONDER ON THIS:

How have those who you have met on your life's journey, connected to your purpose?

_____

_____

_____

_____

_____

_____

Do you know each person's role in your life (including family members)?

_____

_____

_____

_____

_____

UNDERSTAND WHO YOU ARE IN GOD

Each one of us as I mentioned earlier, was created in God's image and after His likeness to be a representative and representation of Him on earth. Each one was created for a specific purpose and to each person, God give specific talents that will equip you to survive and thrive while fulfilling the purpose. He also provides strength to carry on daily. He provided the Holy Spirit who is part of Him as a guide to help you and I focus on the task and not fall short of His glory. The connection was not meant to be turned off at any point in our journeys but to help us become more awakened and aware of our God-given assignments.

Who you are in God is your whole being and self...spirit, soul, mind and covered with flesh (your body and outward appearance). Your DNA is orchestrated by God and cannot be altered. However, due to the sinful nature, culture and tradition into which you were born, you end up losing sight of who you are and gaining sight of who the world wants you to be. The world leads you to connect to the flesh by deluding your mind (thoughts) and allow your soul to crave for temporary wants that will only satisfy temporary pleasures. Your relationship with God should set the foundation for every other relationship you develop. Without building on this solid foundation, you will find yourself on shakable and murky grounds and water. This is the reason you face challenges and struggles...finding yourself live in a chaotic state of mind and yet cannot figure out why things are the way they are.

Building daily by communing with God establishes you and connects your spirit, mind and soul. All work together to ground you in the things and will of God. You are able to hear Him more clearly and know when to seek His face for help.

PONDER ON THIS:

How is your relationship with God at the moment? Are you rooted deeply in Him and able to heed the warning signs or obtain clarity in times of need?

_____

_____

_____

_____

_____

_____

Do you fully understand what it means to be created in God's image and after His likeness?

_____

_____

_____

_____

_____

_____

What are your plans to improve on your relationship with God and what goals are you going to set to help you accomplish these plans?

_____

_____

_____

_____

_____

_____

[60]

WHO ARE YOU?

Taking a deeper dive into who God created you to be, is very essential to living purposefully and truthfully. Who do you say you are? Who do others say or think you are? Who do you truly believe you are? One of the most longings of humans is intimacy. To have someone to hold, cuddle up with, share the good and bad times and make love to. This is the human desire that often leads you towards becoming broken but in the process of losing who you are, you are led to finding the true you God created...your highest self.

Intimacy starts with you building a solid relationship with God by allowing Him to show you what love truly means. Once you have established this foundation, you will become aware of who you are and who God truly created you to be.

You will realize that the world will try to make you into someone else so that you deviate from your purpose and exist than live. You will cut corners by looking for the fastest and shortest route to getting to your destination but you cannot cut corners when God has a Master Plan for your life. Without God, you are nothing and without fulfilling the purpose for which He created you, you only exist. Without knowing who you are, you will live for who others believe you are but inside of you, is your heart longing to be in unison with your soul and mind...to guide and order your steps towards your calling.

Sarai was Abram's wife, who had been barren but found favor in God's eyes. She received the news that she will become a mother at her old age but did not know who God said she was. She could not comprehend her real identity when

God changed her name to Sarah and told her she will bring forth a child. She did not fully connect to God so she allowed her thoughts to become derailed and this led her to make decisions outside of God's plans for her (Genesis 16). She decided to invite her maidservant, Haggai, to take her place and sleep with her husband, Abraham. She was not patient enough to take hold of the promise God made. She did not realize that Gods' promise required "waiting." Haggai, later gave birth to Ishmael but God showed Sarah mercy and gave her a son, Isaac, the child God had promised her when He changed her name and made His plan known to her and Abraham.

How often do you lose your identity while trying to please others and settle for who think you are? How impatient are you with yourself? Do you fail to wait on God for His plan and purpose to come to fruition in your life?

_____

_____

_____

_____

_____

_____

Your true identity is in God through Christ. No one else can define you, outside who God says you are and created you to be.

No one else can live the life God planned and purposed for you. You may have lost your way and feel robbed due to the conditioning of your mind but it is time to reconnect with the you God created and live to fulfill your purpose. You will face trials but you have to always remember who and whose you are. Jesus was tempted by the devil and He reminded him of His true identity. Daniel (book of Daniel) was able to recognize who and whose he was when he was thrown in the lion's den for failing to compromise his faith in God.

Is Your Partner Really from God?

Finding a partner is great but you have to ensure the partner is the one God created for you. Turning your desires into God's reality and blessings, is putting things into your own hands and playing the role of God in your life. You may later begin to complain and find all the reasons in the world, why your partner is problematic. Loneliness can drive you into the arms of a partner but you may faintly hear your inner man...the Spirit of God within you, give you all the warning signs. However, if you do not know who you are, you will ignore the warning signs and agree with what your soul longs for and your thought-based illusions and fantasies.

You may follow your flesh and lust after your partner, become infatuation and fall in love than love him or her for who God made them to be (not what you want them to be). You have to remember that, *"Every good and perfect gift is from above, coming down from the Father of the Heavenly Lights, who does not change like shifting shadows"* – James 1:17. *"The blessings of The Lord, it makes rich, and He adds no sorrow to it"* – Proverbs

10:22. God brought Adam and Eve together. They were the first people created but it has not changed God's plan for you and your partner. Eve was created when Adam was put to sleep. God took out a rib from his side to create Eve. Adam woke up and immediately recognized Eve as part of him.

There was a divine connection between the two of them. The partner God created for you will never let you question your relationship or make you chase him or her. Your partner will recognize you the moment you meet. There will be no egoism or doubt. Your soul, mind and heart (spirit) will connect. One of the reasons why there is so much chaos in relationships today is because we do not allow God in at the beginning. We allow our emotions, ego, culture and tradition dictate the way we go about finding a partner. It is very important that you allow God guide you as a single man or woman during the waiting period.

Learn to find and love yourself, establish and be ready. Adam was placed in the garden of Eden. He had a job. He was single and connect to God on a spiritual and intimate level. He was complete and whole. He could do everything by himself. God saw that he did not have someone of his kind and decided to create Eve as a helpmate. She was created for a purpose. Her purpose and Adam's were aligned with God's purpose for their relationship. She was the suitable helper God created for him. God brought Eve to Adam as his 'wife' (Genesis 2).

Biblical relationships began with a single man meeting a single woman (the helpmate). The man approaches her family with the aim of marrying her. Love was not something that was awakened by emotions. The single man had self-control and respected a woman he loved. There was no jumping into bed and having sex to get him or her to love you and take your relationship to the next level.

The man's intention was well known by the woman and her family. You have to be ready to be the right person for your future spouse. You both have to become committed to one another for intimacy to take place. The man initiates the relationship and as a woman you respond with your requirements and patiently wait for him to meet them one hundred percent, hence, Proverbs 18: 22, *"He who finds a wife finds what is good and receives favor from the Lord."*

A man finds you and you both get to know and understand each other. You have to ensure your purposes align and you are spiritually connected. He will not lust after you because he respects you. *"Do not lust in your heart after her beauty or let her captivate you with her eyes"* – Proverbs 6: 25. God created you for one partner but without you knowing who you are, you find yourself experimenting and going from one relationship to another without meeting that one person. Giving in to lust and becoming broken is a choice you make and you will have to deal with the consequences if your partner is not from God. If your partner is from God, you will not have to compromise who you are for lustful pleasures.

Your partner will have the fear of God and will protect and honor you. Your partner will hold on to the instructions given in 1 Thessalonians 4: 1-8 about sexual immorality. Your partner will understand that your body is the temple of God and will not allow you compromise or defile God's temple. You both will be spiritually connected and committed. He or she will honor your purpose and you both will establish the vision and purpose for your relationship with God as the center of it all. This is why it is important to find who you are and wait for the partner God created you for and from.

PONDER ON THIS:

How is your partner's purpose aligned with yours?

_____

_____

_____

_____

_____

_____

What vision has God given you both for your relationship?

_____

_____

_____

_____

_____

_____

Notice from the story of Adam and Eve that they were not ashamed of who they were. They knew each other well. There was no superiority or inferiority. They were one. Their relationship had no hiccup until the serpent showed up to distort what God had established. A third party destroyed what God had established through deception. Who are you allowing into your relationship? Who is making the decision about who your partner should be or not be? Are you allowing yourself to fall for everyone but forgetting that God created only one helpmate for you?

Allowing God to lead you to your partner that He created for you while waiting, will help you make the right choices that would not result in negative consequences. Pay more attention to your inner strength and voice (the Spirit of God within...in your heart) and less attention to what the world is offering you outside of God's will for your life. Do not allow anyone pressure you to find a spouse. Always remember that God has a purpose for your life and the partner He created for you, will be aligned to that purpose. You will know when you meet. Your spirit, soul and mind will connect and the Spirit of God within you will confirm it.

The Friendships

People come into your life and leave for a season but building friendships that are not in line with God's vision and plan for your life can take you off track and you may never realize it. You may become entangled in their patterns and way of life and forget your own purpose in life. You have to ensure you know your purpose so that those who come into your life are aware of it and are those whose purpose align with yours. Deep can call unto deep and iron can sharpen iron.

> *If you find yourself in the midst of those*
> *who do not share your life's purpose/vision,*
> *it will not be long before you become caught*
> *up in their patterns and ways.*

You will find yourself shifting away from your spirituality into the fleshy ways of life. Allowing yourself to be in tune with the Spirit of God and testing every spirit (remember, we all are spiritual beings covered with flesh that will waste away) to see if they are from God to help you with your purpose or to distract you from it – 1 John 4: 1.

Always allow the Holy Spirit to guide and lead you. Do not allow your emotions to run ahead but learn to control them so that you are able to decipher the truth from the illusions that may be created in your thoughts and the fantasies that may arise and lead you to become emotionally distracted. If you have been broken and have not taken the time to heal, you will find yourself surrounded by friends who are in the same space of pain and will only attract those in pain. Know that when you are going through the hard times, God always shows up through someone who will speak the truth to you in love but if you are still hurting, you will not be able to receive the truth and those you have in your circle will encourage you to discard the truth.

Your ego is awake at this stage, preventing you from accepting what is real. Those who stop you from receiving the truth are part of your purpose stoppers and are only in your life for that reason. However, when you choose to align your ways with those of God and prayerfully invite others into your life, you will be able to separate those who are acquaintances from those who belong in your inner circle or those who are distractions.

CHALLENGE

Go through your list of friends and see who is an acquaintance, a distraction, a purpose helper, a purpose pusher or a purpose stopper. Considering your results, reevaluate your friendships and place everyone in the appropriate categories.

Know who to confide in and who to keep at arm's length. What did you learn during this exercise (be truthful to yourself when going through the list without allowing your emotions play a part in your decision making)?

_____

_____

_____

_____

_____

What life lessons can you take away from this challenge in terms of those who you call friends?

_____

_____

_____

_____

_____

THE LESSONS

We learn so many things after a breakup, divorce, facing tough challenges or loss of a loved one. We may ask all the why, the how's, the what ifs and when questions.

Your mind may race and try to unravel the mysteries behind everything that happened and forget about the lessons that each situation holds. It may be that you needed to try something or there was a need for growth. It may be time for you to gain an awareness of the next season of your life. However, doing to your upbringing and societal pressures, you may think you failed but reality is that without that experience, you may never learn the keys to succeeding. Failures help us realize our strengths and awakens us to see the possibilities in impossible situations.

> *Without failing at something, you will
> never learn to master how to become better
> at it. Failure is the key to becoming
> successful in life.*

You cannot ignore the lessons and believe that you will turn out better in the future.

Learn to master a technique after failing, gives you the edge over those who do not try at all. You have to realize that you do not know it all and having the opportunity to get back up is a God-given gift. It will lead you to rise again. *"Though he falls, he shall not be utterly cast down for The Lord upholds him with his hand"* – Psalm 37:24. The lessons from a breakup or divorce will prepare you for what you need going forward. The end of a friendship will bring to your awareness who to connect with.

LOOKING BACK OR NOT

In order for you to identify the lessons from painful experiences, you have to learn to trace your steps back and ask yourself questions that will assist you in un- covering them. You will have to examine each experience. What was it like at the beginning? When did things start going down? Did you compromise your being? Did you settle due to loneliness? Did you allow your emotions take charge? Was it infatuation or lust? What did you learn overall?

_____

_____

_____

_____

_____

_____

Write down the answers as they come to mind. As you begin to journal, do not try to ask yourself the why questions. Do not let your thoughts make you think of regrets. There are no regrets in life...only lessons that equip you for the future. Everything you have gone through...all those experiences, can only result in your growth as you begin to learn the lessons. Do not look back and dwell on the memories that you want to hold on to but look back, realize the lessons and learn from them. You have to learn to let go of the memories that keep bringing you pain. You have to learn to focus on using the lessons learned from each experience and build on becoming a better not bitter you. You can learn how to improve on the quality of your relationship going forward once you learn the lessons.

You may be wondering what is important about the lessons. Without the lessons, you will continue to repeat patterns and there will never be a change. It will only be a case of putting icing on a cake that you know tastes bad and no one will eat. The longer you hold on to the pain, the more time it will take for you to heal and learn the lessons. The truth is that God never intended for us to carry on with the pain but due to the disconnection between the physical and spiritual being, the mind finds itself in a strange place and processes the pain along with the negative emotions.

There will be times when looking back will serve no purpose but you have to keep moving when you become aware of such times. The Prodigal Son stepped outside of God's purpose for him. He wanted to enjoy life and took his inheritance from his father. He went on to lavish everything and ended up in the pigs' stall and eating with them. He later came to the awareness of who he was and returned to his father (Luke 15: 11-32). You sometimes will have to find your way back to God...back to Love and allow Him to restore you to who He created you to be.

You will realize that all the lessons you learn during your looking back leads you back to God. You will come to understand that trying to do it all on your own or through the influence of others may not get you back to Him. The time has come to go back home to the Source of Life. The one who made you, formed you in the palms of His hands and called you by name. You cannot keep focusing on what is gone. Lot's wife did that and became a pillar of salt (Genesis 19: 15-26). God had instructed her and her husband not to look back but she did.

> *You cannot keep looking back because God's purpose for your life does not exist in the past.*

You may have fallen off the wagon but He is ready to restore you and direct your path. The relationship may have ended but the lesson in it is that you realize the areas of growth going forward. God will not give you half-baked cake that you cannot feed on. The relationship may not have been God's will for you. It relationship may not hold the vision God planned for you. This is why you must let go, heal, forgive yourself and move forward in newness.

As you begin to learn the lessons, you will observe how many times you have repeated patterns and cycles. A relationship usually starts with four people instead of the two individuals who God designed it for: the two individuals coming together and two personas they created as a result of not knowing who they are, lack of a vision or commitment or not healing form painful or broken relationships. Both parties come into the relationship trying to control, manipulate or expect their partners to behave in a certain manner. These two personas are usually birthed out of the illusions, fantasies and unrealistic expectations.

Ego happens to be involved in such cases and fear plays a part as a form of defense mechanism. You may have been broken before your new relationship, but you need to realize that your new partner has nothing to do with the old one who is no longer in your life.

You cannot hold them accountable for something they did not do or know about. You cannot begin to evaluate people from your pain points. If you do not take time to heal, you will realize that doing the above mentioned, may lead you to begin exhibiting narcissistic behaviors. Your heart becomes hardened and you can no longer hear the Holy Spirit within you. You begin to operate from the physical realm: the soul and mind. The truth is that you cannot change anyone.

You cannot continue to self-inflict pain on yourself. You have to learn to let go, hold on to the lessons and understand that no one is ever going to be perfect. You however, have to pay attention and know who will complement you. You have to ensure that your visions align with God's purpose for both of you.

The lessons also serve as a good guide to finding yourself. Remember, life is all about relationships and they help create an awakening to something dead within you that needs to evolve and lead to your growth.

PONDER ON THIS:

In what ways do you envisage using the lessons learned going forward?

_____

_____

_____

_____

_____

_____

THERE IS PURPOSE IN YOUR PAIN

Everything you went through or may be going through in life, always leads you towards your purpose. You may see pain as suffering but in it, lies the answers that will enlighten you and open you to a new season in your journey. Life's best lessons are learned during the most painful experiences. Knowledge is gained, your vision becomes clearer and growth occurs, when you observe and learn from the lessons. Pain serves as a form of test of your faith in God or an avenue to draw you back into His presence so that you can obtain strength to pull through the most difficult times.

Joseph as a teenager, got a glimpse into his purpose and was quick to share his God-given purpose with his brothers who later sold him into slavery out of anger and envy. They plotted and lied to their father that Joseph was killed. They did not know that they were setting him up in line with his purpose. Can you imagine your younger brother narrating a dream about how he will someday rule over you? What will be your reaction? How angry will it make you become? What actions will you take? How would you handle such a situation?

_____

_____

_____

_____

_____

_____

They became angry and allowed their irrational thinking and emotions lead them to selling off their sibling into slavery. They were not able to control their emotions or thoughts.

You must learn to tame your emotions and thoughts...do not let your thoughts and emotions tame you.

Joseph found favor in the eyes of his master and was put in charge of Potiphar's household. Potiphar's wife tried to seduce him and he landed in jail where he met the kinsmen. He interpreted their dreams and later interpreted the king's dream which landed him into his purpose. The dream God had given to him as a teenager was now becoming real. Joseph had dreamt of ruling over his brothers.

God had planted him in his purpose which must have caused him pain but at the end of the day, Joseph fulfilled his purpose and reunited with his siblings who ended up bowing down to him (Genesis 38-40).

Like Joseph, you may be facing tribulations. You may have been rejected, you may be broken or divorced. You may feel rejected but you are not defeated. Everything you are going through and learning from is leading you towards your purpose.

The Prodigal Son realized he had to go back to the Father. He had to return to purpose. God does not count the years you have lost. To God, a day is like a thousand years and a thousand years like a day (2 Peter 3:8). God restores all that you have lost and helps you start over. He forgives you and does not remember the past...He erases the past. You do not have to hold yourself hostage of the past but you can allow the lessons learned to teach you about what lies ahead. God has a purpose for you to fulfill as you make use of the lessons learned.

CHALLENGE

Are you able to identify your purpose in the pain? Are you able to connect the lessons learned with your purpose? Write down what comes up for you. What plans do you have to make to accomplish your purpose?

_____

_____

_____

_____

_____

_____

HEALING THROUGH THE LESSONS

The healing process is not so easy. It will reopen the wounds you have covered up for so long. During my healing process, I thought I was done but I had to go back to reevaluate and address everything. The wounds I did not heal from showed up in form of anger, resentment and bitterness, thus resulting in more pain. I discovered I was still repeating some patterns and cycles. I had not yet learned the lessons I need in those circumstances. As I began to heal from each situation, I became less angry and resentful. I grow to embrace than defend. I held on tightly to the lessons as I watched myself become better not bitter.

It is very vital that you learn the lessons so that you can begin to heal. Without learning the lessons after a breakup or divorce, you will carry on the image of your ex with you. You begin to look for similarities in a new partner. You find your-self attracted to people who are in pain and remind you of your ex. The same issues you had not healed from start to show up in your new relationship and result in chaos. Unreal-istic expectations you laid from your hurt or pain, will only lead you into the arms of someone who will break you fur-ther. Healing not only helps you get rid of bitterness, anger, etc., but also results a spiritual awakening in your mind, soul and heart. You begin to gain clarity about the actions that led to your previous experiences.

The truth about relationships is that you will never find a perfect partner but you will find the one God created for you. You will not find your God-given partner if you allow your ego to step in or when you do not know what you need. You have to realize that without your vision and require-ments aligning to your partner's, conflict will arise and there will be lot of chaos that calmness. You have to see your part-ner through God's lenses. You have to guard your heart so that you do not give yourself to everyone and forget who you are and what you are made of. Are you both spiritually com-patible? Are your values aligned? Can you both sharpen each other and speak life to one another?

You have to learn to guard your heart where the Holy Spirit resides so that you do not become entangled with someone else's rib or helpmate. You have to control your emotions and not allow them interfere with your connection with your heart. You have to think with your heart and not with your head. Your mind (thoughts) may wander off with imagination but your heart will help you obtain clarify and focus on God's will for your life. Your mind allows you to create illusions that lead to worry, anger, bitterness and more but the moment you decide to heal, you will begin to renew your mindset and as you spend time with God, your thoughts will shift towards the will of God. You will hear your inner voice more loudly and you will be able to decipher who is who in your life.

Understanding the
Healing Process

The healing process is not a one-time affair. It is gradual and continuous. You have to be determined to want to heal. You have to be ready to take a look at all the things you have shoved underneath the rug. You have to be prepared to address the most painful incidences...the childhood pain, the rejection, the brokenness, the abuse or loss of a loved one. You have to remember that pain has a domino effect when not addressed. You will need to seek solitude and separate yourself from others. You have to be ready to allow God heal you. You have to be ready to obtain clarity and guidance to continue on your journey (Psalm 23: 2-3). As you uncover the hidden pain, you may become more broken...this will allow you to experience the purification and refinement process needed to become who God created you to be.

I began my healing process by examining my past and digging into the word of God...the blueprint for our lives. The more I buried myself in it, the more I was able to connect the dots and find the answers to all the missing puzzles. God began to show me the mess I created from the childhood pain I carried. There were nights I wept, yelled, laughed and cried more. I grew up in a home of preachers...my great grandfather, grandfather and father were all preachers. I was literally raised in the church and took part in most activities. There was however, polygamy and infidelity in the family. I did not like any of it but I did not have a choice but to be part of the family. My stomach will churn at the thought of it.

There was love in the family but my heart was in pain for the lifestyle that was outside of the godly principles I stood by. I began to find the missing piece of the puzzle that left a void in my soul. My painful divorce brought me to my knees. I had tried on five different occasions to make things work but nothing changed. Do not get me wrong, my ex-husband is a great man in his own stead (we have become friends over the years) but he was the one who was destined to show me what I needed to do to find myself. I never saw the divorce coming and never will wish it for anyone. I had to get out to save my life. I had to find ways to remain strong. I had to learn to find myself. I allowed God to humble me and show me who He really created me to be. I had to connect with my God-given purpose and live!

The Healing Process

There are three stages of the healing process: the shredding, the wringing and the release stages.

THE SHREDDING STAGE

This is the beginning of the healing process. The stage where you start to examine everything underneath the rug. It may rip you apart as you uncover the pain. You have to touch on everything from the past, dissect each one and deduct the lessons.

As you learn to hold on to the lessons, you begin to let go of the past. Let me assure you that it will not be an easy process but be so determined to be committed to the process if you are planning to move forward and become free. You cannot do this in a day. It may take you weeks or months, depending on how you deal with issues and process things. Not everything will have a lesson and you do not have to hold on to anything. You however need to document the lessons.

You may not get closure for everything but do not spend too much time dwelling on what is gone. Your focus should be on the following questions:

What did this teach me about myself? What am I supposed to learn from this experience? As you begin to examine each situation, write down what comes up for you.

_____

_____

_____

_____

_____

_____

What was the pain, the lesson, what did you do wrong or right? How did your partner react to your behavior? What do you need to stop doing or start doing right? What will you tolerate or not tolerate going forward?

———————————————————————————

———————————————————————————

———————————————————————————

———————————————————————————

———————————————————————————

THE WRINGING STAGE

Everything you uncovered during the shredding stage and documented will squeeze the life out of you during the wringing stage. You may have tears rolling down your eyes as you read through your notes. You may feel as if the situation is being reenacted before your eyes. You will get emotional as you begin to realize that you could have learned the lessons earlier than now. This stage will bring you to gain a conscious awareness of all you had denied and deprived yourself of. You are now becoming aware of the truth and reality begins to sink. The truth may hurt you but you are beginning to become free and heal from your past. You have to begin to forgive yourself as the truth is revealed. Slowly release the pain and let go.

Begin to document everything you need to stop doing and the actions steps you will take going forward. Begin to own your truth and learn to stop blaming others for your actions.

There is nothing as knowing the truth and releasing the pain that has held you bound for a long period. You may find yourself staying awake for some days during this stage. I found myself awake journaling down my lessons and rereading them to myself. As I read through each one, I would laugh at the silly things I did without realizing how disconnected I was from myself. The knowledge you can gain from this stage is priceless.

THE RELEASE STAGE

Learning to let go is a challenge we all face but without releasing everything to God, we will hold ourselves in bondage. The release stage helps you understand why God's arms are always there to receive you and help you heal from painful experiences.

Jesus reminded us of where we need to be when we are going through the difficult times of our lives in Matthew 11: 28, *"Come unto me, all ye that labor and are heavy laden, and I will give you rest."* This stage is the resting stage...resting in God to obtain peace of mind and freedom from pain.

> *Releasing the past into God's hands frees you from the painful memories you held on to for so long.*

You not only release the pain but you also get to release the emotions tied to the memories. You become lighter and in the process, begin to forgive yourself for not knowing better...for compromising who you are with who you thought you were. Releasing everything into God's hands also helps you declutter and decondition your mind.

The budding flower starts with a closed bud and gradually opens up while releasing it's petals and exposing its beauty to the world. As you being to heal, you gradually open up and become free of hurt, resentment, pain, anger and bitterness. The heaviness is lifted from your shoulders, you no longer become anxious or overwhelmed with worry. You regain your strength and connect with peace. You begin to understand how forgiveness liberates you. You learn how to fully embrace God's mercy and grace daily. As you remain still in solitude before God, you clearly hear His voice and feel Him soothe your pain.

You realize you were never rejected or broken, you just needed to connect with your spirituality and find yourself. You understand that it was not about you alone, it was about the purpose you needed to become aware of. Everything you went through can help others who you come across, those who may be experiencing similar situations. You are being equipped to become an expert in those areas so that you can sow a seed and save someone in the future.

As you reflect on what you have gone through or may be going through, ask yourself this question, "What is the purpose of this pain?" Write down and reflect what comes up for you. Remember it may take you back in time to connect the dots to where you are now.

_____

_____

_____

_____

_____

_____

Understanding and Focusing on Forgiveness

Forgiveness allows you to embrace the healing process. Your ability to understand forgiveness liberates you from every guilt, shame and pain of the past and allows you to fully embrace God's mercy and grace daily. Without forgiving yourself, you will not be able to forgive others. It is very important you learn to forgive yourself after the release stage of the healing process. How does the pain you hold on to serve you? How does it contribute to your growth? What has it taught you about yourself? What are some of the things you have learned from it that cannot be repeated?

_____

_____

_____

_____

_____

_____

The moment you obtain clarify from those questions, you

begin to realize that you have only held yourself bound so long from the hurt or pain not necessarily the person who hurt you but the actions that resulted from their behavior towards you. You have to remember that they may also have pain deep within that is beginning to ooze out to the surface subconsciously or unconsciously without an awareness of what they need to heal from. This is the reason why you have to forgive yourself first. For not knowing this and your putting yourself in that position. Secondly, you have to forgive yourself because you did not fail but you gained knowledge towards becoming a better you and towards moving forward and to a newer level of yourself. This is what growth is all about. It may not look directly like growth to you but it definitely is.

Take a look at the plants. You plant a seed. It can become trampled upon or uprooted by squirrels hunting for food. It may fall on the road side and you thought it would never grow. You suddenly notice after a few weeks or months that it has grown into a shrub or tree. It had to go through some hardship...people trampling over it, the landscaper mowing the lawn or the squirrel displacing it. There may be heavy rain storms that wash it off the original place you planted it but it still forces itself to push through. You cannot give up because someone showed you who they are. It is part of the process.

Forgiving yourself also sets the pace for which you forgive others. It opens you up to seeing things from a different perspective.

Forgiveness sets you free from the emotional pain and anger or resentment that locks you up as a prisoner of your own thoughts.

This is the beginning of forgiveness. You learn to release every hurt or pain, you learn to forgive yourself and others.

What comes up for you when you think about a situation where someone hurt you?

_____

_____

_____

_____

_____

_____

Forgiveness allows you to shift your perception from pain to reality and results in you breaking the barriers of hurt and emotional pain. Without making an attempt to forgive yourself and others, your pain will ooze out when you interact with others and lead you to hurting them in the process. Remember that no one is in charge of your feelings but you. No one can heal from your pain but you. You have to move through those emotions and memories of pain to get beyond the pain and return to love.

Forgiving Your Body and Mind

It is important to forgive your body. For subjecting your body to abuse so that you can begin to feel free of the toxins generated from the anger, bitterness and hurt. The more you forgive your body, the more relaxed you become. Your mind is where all the pain resides. This is what allows you to create illusions in your thoughts. You have to gradually release your mind and free your soul and body from the hurt and emotional pain you have carried for so long.

This is not a one-time process but it is gradual and you have to be patient if you plan on becoming completely free. This is how you master forgiveness and practice it on daily basis.

Think about the pain in your body. Sometimes, it is not a sickness but the weight carried by your thought process that results in the abuse and subjection of your body to pain. As you begin to write down all the scenarios that have resulted in you becoming hurt, broken or in pain, note what comes up...the thoughts, the illusions, the anger or the resentment and write everything down. How did those things you wrote down affected your health?

_____

_____

_____

_____

_____

_____

Create a list of those you need to forgive and those you need to forgive you. Write down each incidence you are seeking for forgiveness on. What does it feel like to read through the list? What there any relieve or reenactment of the situation?

_____

_____

_____

_____

_____

What goals will you set to ensure that you seek for forgiveness from others and what timeline are you going to set to accomplish this task?

_____

_____

_____

_____

_____

What are your plans to forgive others and yourself? What does that look like and what period are you looking to get this done?

_____

_____

_____

_____

_____

NUGGET 7

UNDERSTANDING UNCONDITIONAL LOVE

To love unconditionally requires lot of work on your part and allows you to see yourself through God's eyes. You are created in God's image and after His likeness. He provided you with the Holy Spirit from birth...your intuition, as a guide and teacher so that you do not go astray or become stuck in life's journey. God had tried everything before giving His Only Son, Christ Jesus, as Savior, to keep man in His Will but man after the fall of Adam, began to wander away from God and into the things of the world. This is how unconditional love operates. It involves giving without expecting anything in return. It does not get puffed up or tries to impress. In giving love, you come to learn more about sacrifice, compassion, loyalty, truth, communication and trust (to mention a few).

God created the first man, Adam and placed in the garden of Eden, God's presence. There was nothing to distract him from God's presence. Adam daily communed with God and could hear Him clearly without interference. The relationship was established between God and man. This set the pace for the most important relationship and learning about unconditional love. The deeper your relationship with God is, the more you learn and understand unconditional love and the more you can love yourself before giving the love you have experienced to others.

You will also build on your confidence as you build up and on your relationship with God. You will taper off egoism and become humble and authentic. You will no longer be angry or remain fearful. You will no longer play victim. You will no longer have desires and wants but realize your focus should be on intentions and needs. Your life will become transformed and you will gain the spiritual awareness that old wine cannot be placed in new wineskin.

LOVING YOURSELF

Would you truly say you love yourself? How do you know if you do? How have you showed yourself love in your relationship (romantic, dating or marriage)? How can you know if your partner truly compliments you (if this is the rib you belong to...the one God knitted you with from the inception)?

_____

_____

_____

_____

With relationships, you have to be the partner you wish to be with. Everything you long for in a partner, should be the very things you need for yourself and you are. You were created as GOOD from the first day God began to create you. You have to fully know and understand who you are to be able to truly love yourself for who God created you to be. To begin learning about yourself and become the love you are created to be, you have to understand that conformity to the world cannot be manifested in you. Your mind has to be constantly renewed (Romans 12: 2).

Let us take a look at understand how to fully love yourself from 1 Corinthians 13: 4-8: "Love is patient, love is kind. It does not envy, it does not boast, it is not proud. It does not dishonor others, it is not self-seeking, it is not easily angered, it keeps no records of wrong. Love does not delight in evil but rejoices with the truth. It always protects, always trusts, always hopes, always perseveres. Love never fails." Love is patient. How patient are you with yourself? How much time do you spend without rushing to get to know your true self? How often do you rush in making the decisions that pertain to your life and growth?

_____

_____

_____

_____

_____

_____

Love is kind. How kind are you to yourself? You have to be able to give yourself kindness before sharing it with others. Others may let you down, mistreat you or hurt you but your ability to share kindness does not stop based on their attitude towards you. Your true essence allows you to give the kindness to others because it is part of who you are.

Love does not envy. Do you spend time envying others based on their progress or success, relationship or career? If you answered yes, there are still some areas you need to work on. You are made of love and you are love. You do not have to envy others because you know that everyone was created with different gifts (talents) and what someone else has does not change who you are or make you see yourself less than who you are. No one can take what God has given to you.

Love does not boast. You do not see yourself outside of who God made you. You do not see your achievements as something you worked on by yourself because it was all part of God's gift to you. Whatever your accomplishments, you should become more humbled by what God will do through you and those things. You glorify God with those and not yourself.

Love is not proud. It is humble. It does not seek after itself. It freely gives without expecting anything in return. For you to operate as the love God created you to be, you have to be able to give to others the love you are without expecting them to reciprocate.

The moment you start to expect something back in return, it becomes a transaction and is no longer love.

Love always rejoices in the truth. You cannot lie when it is love or cover it up. If you have to cover up or lie about it, it will be filled with infatuation and lust coupled with negative emotions that will lead to hurt or pain.

Love always protects. Do you protect yourself by setting boundaries or do you allow everyone into your space only for them to hurt you and leave you in pain and anger? What can you do to change this going forward?

_____

_____

_____

_____

_____

Love does not dishonor others nor is it selfish. The nature of humans based on the conditioned mind is selfishness. The conditioned mind always sets expectations based on what it can get from others and when those expectations are not met, he or she begins to dishonor others. You cannot operate from this space when you truly love yourself. Love has nothing to do with manipulating or controlling others.

Love does not expect to receive but delights in giving. Love always trusts. How much do you trust yourself? You cannot trust others if you have not learned to trust yourself. You will only look for others to entrust with what you need do for yourself and when they let you down, you become hurt or broken. The more you find yourself, the more trust you have for yourself. Love always hopes and perseveres. Hope has to do with trust. Trusting God and putting your hope in Him. Trusting His Timing while believing that those things you do not see but you speak in faith, will manifest in due season. Hope is a virtue that operates with perseverance. The world will teach you to run the rat race and you will end up in a mouse trap but understanding that you have to trust God, persevere and have hope while patiently waiting for your breakthrough, will lead you to gain wisdom of how God operates with you in love and how you can through that process, love your journey and self in return.

Love is freely given. You do not have to show it. Trying to show it to others will only make you love for attention and try to impress them. You give love and do not have to chase to get or give it. The other person must be ready to receive it. If he or she is not ready, you will be wasting your time with the wrong person. "God so loved the world that He gave His Only Son so that whoever believes in Him, will not perish" (John 3: 16). The keyword here is whoever. God gave but did not force love on us. The same applies to relationships. You cannot force anyone to love you but you can give your love to the one who is ready to receive it and give you love in return. Everything outside of this is what the world teaches as fantasy and illusions not love.

The moment you love yourself and become whole, you realize that not everyone will love you and you cannot give love to everyone but to those who are ready to receive the love that you have. This is where you begin to set boundaries so that you protect yourself (as love). You set the pace for which others come into your space. You know what you are willing to allow and disallow. Offenses will arise from your decisions but you have to have principles in place to live in love and in truth. This is how you guard your heart. This is how you stay free from compromising who God made you to be.

No one can receive love when in pain...you cannot give love when in pain.

Spend time loving yourself, becoming whole and complete before trying to give or receive love from others.

IDENTIFYING AND CONNECTING WITH YOUR SPIRIT

Finding yourself involves connecting to the inner spirit...the Spirit of God within you. This is the source of Life and Light in you...the heart that allows God reveal Himself to you. Your spirit allows you to discern between good and evil, right or wrong. You are able to recognize those who are your purpose helpers, purpose stoppers and purpose pushers. You are able to connect with others through discernment and you have mastered who you are, gained awareness of the love that you are and how to treat others when you come in to a relationship or make connections.

The Holy Spirit is your guide, ordering your steps and teaching you how to test every spirit you meet (1 John 4: 1). Without the Holy Spirit fully active within you, you will not be able to discern who is real or not. You will get angry at every situation leading you towards your growth without realizing what the purpose is. Understand that the Holy Spirit is your eye opener, enlightening you to see everything that is dark and bringing them to light so that you can become better, wiser and stronger.

LOVE DOES NOT FOCUS ON THE PAST

You may find loving yourself difficult because of the painful and experiences and memories you are holding on to. The truth is that love does not focus on the past. Love always lives in the present moment and keeps no records of wrongs (1 Corinthians 13: 5). The world, culture and tradition teaches you to hold on to pain and ignore everyone who has hurt you or caused you pain. This is the reason you are bound and haunted by the past. You cannot ignore someone you used to care about deeply, if you are holding on to grudges and hurt. You have to learn to heal and forgive them so that you can become unbound by the hurt, emotions and pain. You will always remember if you choose to but you also have to remember that forgiveness is for you.

Without experiencing forgiveness, your soul is still bound to that partner, that person and the emotional pain will cost you your health some of the time. At that point, the only person you are fighting and struggling with is you.

You are restricting yourself from growing and endless possibilities. The person who hurt may not even remember what happened. It is like you going to shop for clothes after losing weight. You store the bigger sizes in a storage or some place in your closet. After a while, the clothes take on a stale smell and if you happened to store them in a moist closet, they may begin to grow moldy. You may begin to experience respiratory distress but you do not seem to think about the source of your discomfort as something in your closet. That is what it looks like when you hold on to grudges and resentment from the past. You end up choking and getting sick but the other party is living their lives while you are staying miserable. The more you focus on the pain, the longer it will take you to heal and move beyond the painful past.

PONDER ON THIS:

Ask yourself, "Is it worth holding on to the pain?" "Are you the source of your own hurt and pain?" "Could you be contributing to your own health issues without realizing it?"

_____

_____

_____

_____

_____

_____

_____

THE FOUNDATION OF LOVE

Understanding the foundation of love is key to finding yourself. We have been conditioned to believing what love is not and when we do not have the ability to fully connect to love, we will keep seeking validation and attention from others. The truth is God validated you and I when He signed, sealed and delivered us as GOOD. He gave you and I love when He got tired of how the world operated (in hurt, affliction and pain). He sent Christ to show us how to love. He gave His only Son. Love always gives before it can receive. Love does not judge but corrects.

Love does not see your past but your present moment and ways to support you to become better. They brought the adulterous woman to Jesus and wanted to stone her (John 8: 1-11), He asked if any of them had no sin and to cast the first stone. No one was able to do so but all walked away. He looked at her with love and corrected her by telling her to go and sin no more. That is what love does. It does not focus on your past. It is not anything money can buy. It is not sex guaranteed. It is clothed with compassion, kindness, giving, grace, mercy, acceptance, peace and intimacy to mention a few attributes.

Love is not afraid to speak out the truth. It is not associated with fear. Fear is associated with abuse, pain, anger, greed, addiction, selfishness, obsession, resentment and shame. You cannot love anyone if you are operating in any of the fearful spaces listed. "There is no fear in love but perfect love drives out fear because fear has to do with punishment" – 1 John 4: 18. Did you get that? Pain, greed, addiction, selfishness, resentment, shame and obsession all have to do with punishment hence there is no love in it, if any of it exist. The foundation of love cannot be shaken neither can it hold fear. It has and will forever remain solid but you have to understand and tap into it to be able to fully operate from a space of love in your life and relationship. To operate in a space of fear is to be disconnected from who you are...love. You make a shift from love to fear and begin to experience pain as a form of punishment. That solid foundation of love is first established in your relationship with God. The more intimate and grounded you are in that relationship, the less you will connect to fear, hurt, pain, bitterness or resentment. The more you learn to love yourself as the second level of relationship, the more you will value yourself and the less you do the following:

- Seek for acceptance or validation – God has already accepted you when you were created.
- Allow others abuse you – Loving yourself allows you to take charge of your life and say no to abuse or violence of any form. God did not create you to be abused or used but created you as love to be loved.
- Speak death and negativity into your life – The more you love and value yourself, the more you will begin to speak life and the truth God spoke about you, in His promises.

- You will no longer hang around those who cannot speak the truth in love. You will begin to understand that life is not about what is seen, what feels or looks good but about becoming the good and living it out loud.
- You will not focus on what others have to say but on God's will for your life.

You will begin to understand that your life is about purpose and you can only fulfill that purpose when you tune in to God and stay in sync with His will for you.

Love does not set boundaries...it knows no limits...it has no secrets and is always giving. It may be tested but it never fails. It makes you glow and grow. It makes you rich and successful. You must fully experience and understand it before you can connect with your partner and others to share it.

Now that you have gain an awareness of the foundation of love, what have you learned about yourself and how do you plan on loving yourself before others going forward?

_____

_____

_____

_____

_____

_____

UNDERSTANDING DIVINE
RELATIONSHIPS

To be able to comprehend the principles of love, your emotions and purpose, I will walk you through a few relationship scenarios so that you can begin to see and understand how it relates to you. This will help you understand what you have experienced, you are currently experience or will experience late on in your journey.

CAIN AND ABEL – GENESIS 4

How does negative energy and anger operate and lead to consequences that may last a lifetime? It does not take very long to associate with negative energy. Cain was quick to connect to it when God blessed and accepted his brother, Abel's offering.

Can became resentful and plotted to kill his brother. He took Abel's life...he connected to the negative energy, emotions and thoughts and his choices resulted in the consequences he faced (Genesis 4). Like Cain, you may be connecting to negative energy and become resentful and angry. You may begin plotting revenge and eventually carry out the act but have you thought about the consequences that may result due to your actions? Anger leads to you becoming broken. You feel let down, your heart becomes hardened and you go on a raging spree.

Once you are in that space, you will be far away from love or be able to love yourself not to talk of anyone else. Without healing and forgiveness, you cannot reenter into the arena of love and positive thinking. There will be a shift in the trajectory of your life...away from purpose into self-will...away from hearing God speak to you through the spirit in you...away from your true essence and being. You gradually wander off into another world...another space and outside of the life that God created for you.

Cain lost it completely. He failed to see that Abel's journey and purpose was completely different from his. You cannot act out based on the negative energy and emotions.

> *You have to tune in and allow your spirit speak to you...in stillness lies clarity. You have to be able to think before you act and reason before you react.*

You cannot allow your thoughts and emotions lead you astray. This is one of the reasons why you must return to

God. Jesus on the cross cried out when He was in pain asking why God forsook Him but then had to come back to realize His purpose and said, "Not my will but Your will, Lord, be done" – Luke 22: 42.

What is your take away from this nugget so far? What are you going to work on going forward?

_____

_____

_____

_____

_____

_____

How does seduction or lust take your focus of your journey and cause you pain? How do you shift from your purpose and allow your emotions rob you of your truth? Do you return to God and allow Him to restore you?

_____

_____

_____

_____

_____

_____

SAMSON AND DELILAH – JUDGES 14-16

Samson was a man of strength, born into a family that feared the Lord. God had a plan He was going to execute through Samson. Samson was not supposed to marry from the tribe of the Philistines. He however married Delilah who seduced him into giving up his secret. Delilah was paid by the Philistine rulers to get the secret and she manipulated Samson (Judges 14-16). She did what she wanted to do for the money but God had a plan and purpose for Samson. She discovered Samson's strength was connected to his hair lockets and she shaved his head while he was asleep. Samson ended receiving his strength back from God and destroyed the Philistines.

You may sometimes go through pain to understand your purpose in life. It may not make sense to you but it is all part of God's plan to lead you to your purpose. You have to remember that purpose is the only reason you and I were created. You do not know your strength until you reach the bottom. You do not connect with your purpose until you have experienced pain and allowed God to heal and hold you by the hand. It is all about God's Master Plan to use you for His Glory! You cannot find a diamond on the surface, you must go way under to get it. The same applies to pearl. You must get to the bottom of the sea to find the oysters holding the pearls.

Samson realized he had gone astray and he asked God to restore his strength. You have to realize when you hit rock bottom that you need to return to God...Love Himself, and allow Him embrace and restore your strength. You may begin to feel depleted after lust. Your emotions led you in the

wrong direction but you always have the opportunity to dis-
connect, let go and let God renew your strength and revive
your journey. Does this resonate with you? Do you need to
find your strength again? Are you willing to allow God lead
you for the rest of your journey?

_____

_____

_____

_____

_____

_____

RUTH AND BOAZ – RUTH 1-3

You may have lost your spouse and feel the need to be loved
again. You may have experienced a broken relationship or
divorce and need to find love again but how long are you willing to wait?

Ruth had lost her husband and decided to stay with her
mother-in-law, Naomi. She had to go work in the fields so
that they could have food to eat. She landed on Boaz's prop-
erty and he noticed her. Boaz was a rich man who owned the
farm land that Naomi was working on. Boaz singled her out
of the crowd. He inquired about her from his chief officer.
He had done his research before speaking to her. He specifi-
cally told her not to leave his field for another. As a woman, I
want you to understand this part of this story. He inquired of
her then spoke with her. He instructed her not to go some-
where else. Boaz recognized his wife. He did not want her to

leave his vicinity (Ruth 1-3). This is what protection looks like.

A man who needs you in his life...a man who recognizes that you are his missing rib, will not let you leave his presence and will do his homework to know you well before speaking to you. Boaz prayed for her and told her what he found out about her. That man will recognize you as his helpmate and will pray for you when he finds you. This story however took a twist when Naomi instructed Ruth to go lay at his feet at night. Naomi asked Ruth to cover herself with his cloak. This was a no go area and Boaz did not seize the opportunity to sleep with her but respected her and sang her praise while letting her know her value. He listened to her and did as she said. This story is a reminder for singles (both men and women).

> *Love will never rush you but pray with you and reassure you.*

This was part of Ruth and Boaz's story. There was love, prayer, respect and protection. Love will pray with and for you, love will respect and protect you. You do not have to give in and get hurt but you need to learn to wait...love worth having is worth waiting for! Can you see the importance of patiently waiting? Do you understand why love will protect you not harm you? Are you able to understand that love holds no lust or infatuation?

_____

_____

_____

_____

_____

_____

Nabal's Wife and David – 1 Samuel 25: 2-2 Samuel 3: 3

You may find yourself in the wrong relationship and you become aware of who you are, needing to make a shift. Others may not understand it but if it is God's time to plant you in the right place at the right time, nothing will stop His move. He will use you according to the purpose of your creation.

Abigail was Nabal's wife. A man who was wealthy but wicked. Abigail never used her authority for anything negative. Nabal spoke ill of David when he (David) sought to him for favor (1 Samuel 25-2 Samuel 3: 3). Abigail noticed that God was with David. She went behind Nabal and provided David with gifts to make peace and to prevent David from getting angry and committing murder.

God had planted her in that position for such a time. She acted in love not fear or hurt. How often does God plant you in a place but you do not recognize why you are there? How often do you use your position to create chaos than to build on love?

_____

_____

_____

_____

_____

_____

Notice she did not connect to her emotions negatively to act out based on what her husband said about David. She recognized that God was with David and she showered him with favor.

You may find yourself knowing your purpose and talking about it to those who do not want you to move forward. Without recognizing their energy, you may find yourself connecting with it and becoming discouraged with your purpose. How do you plan to make a shift when you find out that you are with the partner who is wrong for you or planning to hurt someone else? Will you join the angry partner in plotting a coup or will you allow your emotions connect with the truth and come to the other party's rescue?

_____

_____

_____

_____

_____

_____

Remember, love does not plot evil but looks out for the good in everyone. What you dish out to others will come back to you someday. Abigail recognized that Nabal was ill-tempered but she knew God was with David. She prevented David from revenging and take things into his own hands. That is what love does.

How often do you recognize where God places you strategically for a purpose? Do you allow your emotions to get in the way and cloud your judgment? Can you decipher when God brings someone your way for a reason and season?

_____

_____

_____

_____

_____

You may receive a vision from God about your life but may not understand it. You may be tested to see if you can grow in faith or if you will compromise your true essence to conform with the tradition, culture and societal norm. How will you stand through it all? Are you able to recognize how your emotions can take you off track your journey of purpose?

_____

_____

_____

_____

_____

Joseph and His Dreams – Genesis 37-39

Joseph as a teenager had dreams about his life and purpose. He got too excited and told his siblings. They were not happy to hear about his dreams and could not seem to accept it. They sold Joseph to slavery out of selfishness. They thought that would stop God's plan for him. They dipped his rob in the blood of a slaughtered goat and presented it to their father to fake his death (Genesis 37, 39-41). Joseph however, ended up in Potiphar's house as second in command. He had another experience with Potiphar's wife who tried to seduce him but failed. Joseph was thrown in jail. He interpreted the dreams of the cupbearer and baker who he thought would help him get out of jail. The time came for him to interpret the King's dream and he became second in command again. His purpose (dreams) was fulfilled.

Joseph never allowed his emotions to sidetrack him or take him off the course of his purpose in life. He did not allow his emotions to cloud his judgement and give in to Potiphar's wife seduction. He did not try to forge ahead but knew that patience was an attribute he had to hold on to. He forgave his brothers at the end of the day because he understood that purpose and love are greater than anything in life. His faith was tested but he stood the test of time. He recognized that his journey was about his purpose. He did not seek out to revenge. He knew God was with him throughout his journey. Through love, forgiveness became an easy thing to do when he saw his brothers.

You have to realize that during the journey of purpose, not everyone can come with you, not everyone will show you love, not everyone will agree with you because it is not their purpose but yours. There will be those who will betray you but you cannot allow them distract you from your course. You have to learn to stay focused while allowing God to lead and guide you along the journey.

You sometimes have to lose the self you are comfortable with (and those who make you comfortable in that environment) to be able to connect to love, walk in patience and live in and with purpose. How are you going to allow all the experiences you have gone through help you connect to the purpose God created you for?

_____

_____

_____

_____

_____

_____

THE ROLE OF CHRIST – HEBREWS 9

In the old testament, atonement for sins was a ceremony performed by the high priest once a year. It involved the sprinkling of the blood of goats and calves on the altar and the people by entering into the Holy of Holies/Tabernacle which were man made. God saw that people continued to live in sin and the atonement process did not really lead to repentance. Hence, He decided to send Jesus Christ to die once and for all for our sins. Christ did not enter a man-made tabernacle but God's throne room of grace, Heaven. His blood for shed for our sins so that we can become redeemed and forgiven. So Christ was once offered to bear the sins of many; and unto them that look for him shall he appear the second time without sin unto salvation (Hebrews 9: 28).

Our relationship with God through Christ, gives us the ability to become free of sin that we may become aware of who we truly are created to be not who the world wants us to be, hence the reason why we must return to love...returning to God (Love Himself) while giving up the sinful nature (knowing Christ has already died so that we can go and sin no more). John 3:16 says, *"For God so loved the world, that He gave His only begotten son...that whoever believes in Him will not perish but have eternal life."* Note three things from this verse: **Loved, Gave, Believes**. God gave Christ because of His love for us (who are created in the same love but have fallen short of the glory of God – His Love sown and shown through us).

Without God loving us, there will be no giving of Christ on the cross. Love is associated with giving but you also have to believe so that you can receive the love. You have to believe in Christ as the ultimate sacrifice for love. Believing leads to you not perishing but having eternal life through Christ in God. Believing in the love of God and the sacrifice of Christ as a gift leads you to adopting the Christ-like nature in humility. The blood of Christ was shed as evidence of God's love to wipe away our sins, take away our unfaithfulness and restore us to the life God originally created for you and I when He looked at each one of us and said, "You Are Good" hence go forth into the world and fulfill your purpose.

The blood of Christ was shed for the forgiveness of our sins. This replaced the yearly purification ceremony performed by the high priest on behalf of the Israelites. The Most Holy Place was not disclosed with the Old Testament because the gifts and sacrifices and sprinkling the blood of goats and calves did not take away the sins of the Israelites since the ceremony applied only to external regulations/cleansing. They were only cleaned outwardly but not internally convinced and free.

Christ offered His blood so that our consciences can be free of sinful acts that lead to death so that we can truly serve the Living God. The blood of Christ wasn't shed as a form of protection or anything else but for the forgiveness of sins. This is the truth that sets us free and convicts us to work out our salvation with fear and trembling.

To live a sinless life this requires a conviction and deep understanding of why Christ urged those who came to Him to "go and sin no more." You can only see others from the perspective Christ did when operating in love. He did not judge or condemn them but spoke life to them in love. He acted in kindness which is an attribute of love. Kindness does not require compensation. It is an act of love and it is freely given. If you have to be compensated for being kind, then you do not know what love is. He did everything with humility not out of ego, pride or fear. He corrected them in love.

Ego speaks from a place of pride and fear.
Judgement comes from a place of pain.
Courage speaks from a place of humility
and correction comes from a place of love.
Where are you operating from?

This is the reason why Paul urged us to be Christ-like in all we do. You can only fully operate in and from a space of love when you are fully aware of who you are in Christ and God with the help of the Holy Spirit. The Love that created you in His image and after His Likeness, can only birth into you the love which you can share with others when you become fully aware of who you are. 1 John 4: 20 states, *"Whoever claims to love God yet hates a brother or sister is a liar. For whoever does not love their brother and sister, whom they have seen, cannot love God, whom they have not seen."*

There are those who will never fully understand the ministry and role of Christ. He demonstrated the reason why the church was not a place of money when He turned the tables and called it a house of robbers. This is what today's church is. It is no longer a place that serves to show the true essence of who God created us to be. It has become a place of business and meetups for storytelling. We often forget that the greatest storyteller in the bible was the devil. He told the convincing story to delude Eve at the beginning of creation. He told the story by giving the Israelites the idea that they needed to create a golden calf to worship even though God was talking them to the promise land. The devil continues to use the fascinating and enchanting stories to entrap people using their emotions (which God gave as a source to reconnect to Him and get wisdom and understanding in times of need). God gave Christ as a sign of the love He has for us. The love in which we were created with and conceived from. The love which we are to share with others when we truly know how and learn how to love ourselves first so that we can love others with the same measure and do unto them as we want done to us.

Your mission in life is to live in love and to be love that will be loved in return while carrying and living out the purpose for your creation. Without knowing this love which God shared through Christ, you cannot live in love or comprehend the fact that you are love to be loved.

Does this awaken something in you? Can you see why it is important to return to love and to God?

_____

_____

_____

_____

_____

_____

UNDERSTANDING THE PRO-CESS

The process is one of the toughest things to deal with in the journey of life. We sometimes look for ways to cut out the struggles but there is a reason for each one. They are there to help us learn to trust God more and seek Him in times of our needs. However, we forget to connect to Him but connect to others to seek for answers. It may be seeking for answers from a pastor to a friend. However, it is important that you recognize and understand how God works in your life to be able to understand the process.

UNDERSTANDING THE STRUGGLES

You sometimes have to face struggles, experience pain and

learn through faith, for you grow and emerge into who God created you to be. This sometimes will be as a result of you trying to do it all on your own but failing to realize you cannot go far without God on your side. It may also be as a test of your faith to see if you will give up on God. Abraham had to face the test when God asked him to sacrifice Isaac. God wanted to see how Abraham will trust Him during the struggles of life. You sometimes need to recognize ow the process works.

> *Pain is part of your growth. Pain is a test of your faith. Pain brings about the spiritual awakening process.*

Pain leads you to connect back to God not man. Learn to hold on to God through and beyond the pain. There is life beyond the pain and there is purpose in your pain. You cannot truly see the beauty of the rose if it had no thorns on its stem. The rose still blossoms through the thorns it holds. It is all part of the refinement process you have to go through to emerge into a stronger, wiser and better you. You cannot fully know how strong you are without the test of time.

The rose will forever thrive in the midst of the thorns. You will survive each trial and emerge a wiser you while you blossom and shine your light. Job had his faith tested but never cursed God in the process. He recognized that it was God who had the power to give and take away as He deemed and created. Abraham had his faith tested when He was asked to sacrifice Isaac but stood in obedience because he understood that God is the giver of everything.

PONDER ON THIS:

What trials are you facing that you do not recognize as part of the process? What do you need to tap into to become obedient and submissive to the process? What level of your faith is being tested and how will you stand the test of time during the process?

_____

_____

_____

_____

_____

_____

Not everything that you think is a loss is LOST. God has the power to give and take away anything and everything that is not part of the process for preparing you to walk in purpose. You have to learn to surrender in obedience to God's Will and purpose for your life. You have to learn to understand the process.

THE TRUTH ABOUT PAIN

Pain if not dealt with can result in crisis. Pain triggers the negative emotions and ego to become awakened in you as a form of self-defense while you are trying to justify the situation to your favor. You may lie to yourself in the process and deny yourself from receiving the truth. You may try hard to cover everything but sometimes it oozes out when you are with those who have healed and owned their own truth while choosing to walk in purpose. You may be surrounded by those who are still holding on to pain or have become numb to pain and who will massage your ego and accept you because they are seeking to impress and hold you back into the same space they are existing and operating from...like the saying, "The more the merrier." You know you are made to feel good but deep inside of you, there is the yearning for something different and you do not really want to be in that space you are in. However, they do not make you feel bad and help you remain in that place of denial and far from the truth that will set you free.

Healing is a process that many may not understand how to go about when in pain. Forgiveness may be something you are struggling with because you do not know how to release the pain. Grudges may be something you are holding on to because others are pushing you to hold back from letting go. However, you need to realize that no one can hold you back from yourself. You have to choose to heal, forgive and let go. You have to realize that sometimes the chastisement is to help you grow. You have to understand that there is a time for pruning so purification can take place.

You need to know that the diamond is not found on the surface but you have to go deep down in the dirt to bring out the diamond to be able to see it sparkle.

What you may deem as pain may not be pain to God. What you may see as uncomfortable may be comforting to God. What you may see as a test may be an elevation in God's eyes. You cannot allow your emotions or fear to see pain as something different but as a means of your growth. You cannot allow your emotions to lead you to becoming bitter rather than better. Everything you go through should lead you back to God to ask for help not to man to gain advise that may lead you further in to experiencing more pain. David recognized that he needed to connect to God every time he was in that place. He wrote in Psalm 121: 1-2, *"I will lift up mine eyes to the hills, where does my help come from? My help comes from The Lord, The Maker of Heaven and Earth."*

Every pain and discomfort you face should lead you back to God...the love of your life. It should lead you to rekindle your relationship with Him. It should lead you to a place of solitude and prayer. This is the only way you can turn your pain into purposeful living by trusting The One who created you and entrusting everything into His care and hands. You will only see this as difficult when you do not see the need to rely on God but others for advice.

You may be drawn to the advice of others and this may draw you further into pain than healing. You need to realize that with God, you are stronger than your pain. There is gain when you learn from your pain. The lessons in the pain awakens you to find the answers that lead you out of the storms. Life is the teacher and without being taught the lessons that you need for your growth, you will keep existing and not live in and with purpose. It is not always about how many years you spent in the relationship or what you have invested. It is not always about what you lost. It is about your growth and life's purpose.

> *Purpose is greater than pain and it is the reason for living and your creation.*

Decisions made out of self-will or gratification may contribute to your pain. Your decisions are based on your choices. Your choices emerge from your thoughts. Your thoughts start with a preconceived idea or illusion that you have marinated. Fear may trickle in and make it worse hence you may end up with a negative consequence to face. You have the choice to learn from the experience but you have to allow God help you get out of your own way while leaving the pain and past behind. You cannot keep focusing on falling bricks and expect things to change.

> *If you are busy focusing on falling bricks, you will never realize they were meant to be stepping stones for you to cross over to the next phase of your journey in life.*

WHY WE FACE SO MUCH STRUGGLES

It is not always pleasant to face struggles and it can be draining, sometimes life threatening and drenching. However, you cannot allow every obstacle to remain a stumbling block without dealing with the situation, facing it and allow it to lead to suffering and depression. The conditioning of your

mind due to the worldly philosophical teachings and tradition can draw you away from God and the path that God has
set before you but you need to recognize some of the reasons
why you struggle.

SETTING UNREALISTIC EXPECTATIONS

You may set unrealistic expectations based on what you want
others to do for you without trying to do it on your own. You
may not trust yourself or your abilities. You may not believe
you can do those things and so you allow others into your
process and give them the power to take a lead in your life
only to be left hurt or disappointed. Without understanding
what you are doing, you will continue to repeat patterns and
eventually feel broken. You have to realize that you cannot
rely on others but you have to learn to trust God while not
leaning on your own understanding (Proverbs 3:5-6). God
already equipped you with all you need but you have to seek
Him for assistance to uncover those hidden gems in your
own life and satisfy those needs on your own.

SURROUNDING YOURSELF WITH PEOPLE IN THE SAME SITUATION

You find it easy to surround yourself with people in the
same situation that massage your ego and do not want you
to get out of the painful space. They provide you with opin-
ions that leaves you further stuck in the process. They
make you believe you are better off where you are even
though you have a longing to get out of that space. You

cannot overcome life's challenges when you choose to stay with those who cannot tell you the truth because they do not live in their own truth. You must take responsibility knowing that you alone are responsible for the consequences you will face or are facing.

You Do Not Want to Talk About the Situation

You seem to shove the situation under the rug and think it does not need to be addressed. You however fail to realize that the more you do this, the more you find yourself repeating patterns. You cannot learn the lessons if you keep avoiding the situation. You will only incur more pain and suffer more consequences. Everything you experience allows you gain knowledge and grow to become who God created you to be. The lessons may be painful but it is the best way to learn through humility while letting go of pride to become better not a bitter version of you. The truth is that pain and love cannot live in the same space. You have to be free by letting go of all the pain that has accumulated over the years and become free to be who God created you to be.

You can never love anyone in pain. You cannot truly love yourself in pain. The more pain you carry, the harder it becomes to love anyone including yourself. Keeping your pain, a secret, mutilates you. You have to learn that there are no secrets in life. Everything will eventually come out and the sooner you begin to heal, the quicker you gain the knowledge and be free of the pain from the struggles.

You Allow Philosophy and Tradition In

You ought to realize that most people in the world today, are searching for answers just like you and I. They may be living in a confused state or living a lie while faking it to make it. However, there may be tons of underlying pain that you do not see or know about. All you may observe is what they are flaunting on the external to soothe their pain or package themselves. Human conditioning is on-going...minute by minute and people may not be able to decipher the truth from the lies. You and I are reminded *to "Continue to live your lives in Him, rooted and built in Him, strengthened in the faith you were taught and overflowing with thankfulness. See to it that no one takes you captive through the hollow and deceptive philosophy which depends on human tradition and the elemental spiritual forces of this world rather than on Christ" – Colossians 2: 6-8.*

You have to guard your heart and allow God set the pace for your life. You have to align your thoughts with your attitude while guarding your heart. Always remember that your attitude is a reflection of your mindset and your mindset is based on what you feed it. What are some of the challenges you are facing and how are you allowing those challenges shape you to become the true you God created?

_____

_____

_____

_____

_____

Dealing with The Consequences of Disobedience

You may ignore your inner man (the voice of God within) or what you call intuition but reality is that there are consequences that come with that. Every thing we do should bring God glory and honor. It should help us establish a better and stronger relationship with God while bonding with His Love. However, there are consequences when we fail to obey or listen to God speak to us.

Adam and Eve had to face the consequences of disobeying God when they ate from the tree of knowledge of good and evil. The began to struggle to survive...tilling the land and laboring in pain to have children. That is where the consequences of disobediences began. The choices you make always lead to consequences that may be hard to deal with. However, owning your truth may help ease of some of the pain from the consequences.

The truth always hits a nerve and makes you uncomfortable but it is reality that you cannot avoid. Dealing with the consequences of disobedience, often takes you through the rough path of life. However, you must learn how to climb out without getting upset or becoming resentful. Always remember that pain is meant to be the teacher that teaches you the lessons that will help you grow in life. Anything that gets you upset or makes you angry reveals a part of your life that needs to grow and uncover but you are not ready to deal with. The truth will often hit a nerve but if your ego is awakened and you are living in fear, you will keep blaming others and running away from your reality.

The truth is an attribute of love that leads to correction after a period of disobedience. Acknowledge and owning the truth about your poor choices. The truth will speak in love and lead you to a place of humility. You will learn to become obedient and embrace correction. You have to learn to become better not bitter. You have to become stronger not weaker. You have to learn to stop playing victim and begin to learn how to be victorious. To truly deal with the consequences of disobedience, you must learn how to stay humble and not be afraid of facing your past.

Know that it is okay to make mistakes otherwise you will not have anything to learn about. It is okay to fail otherwise you will not have the opportunity to try again. Life after all, is about learning and the only way you can learn is to gain knowledge from failed experiences. You have to have a heart of forgiveness to develop new strength to succeed and keep praying for yourself and others along the journey.

Learn to See Through God's Eyes

You have to learn to change the way you think and decondition yourself from all that you have learned in this world. You have to ask yourself every time you have a situation or find yourself in a place contrary to your spirit, "Was God in it or was it just me making those decisions while believing that God was leading me? What I talking myself into a situation? Could I be following my own clouded thoughts out of fear and the illusions I created?" Think about a situation you experienced. Ask yourself these questions and write down your answers.

_____

_____

_____

_____

_____

_____

What did you notice? Was there any decision you made that was yours but you thought was God speaking to you? Did you have to face the consequences? What did you learn from that experience?

_____

_____

_____

_____

_____

_____

You may seek for validation from others but it may leave you stuck. You have to learn to seek God first, embrace your truth and make decisions in line with God's will for you. Looking to others may leave you broken or hurt and this may lead you to hurt others without you knowing that your decisions were off track from God's purpose for you. You need to grasp how God sees you, how He deals with you and how He answers you when you call on Him. This will help you see and understand from His perspective. You may even doubt your existence based on life's experiences. If this happens you need to ask yourself the following questions:

What does God think of me? How does He see me? What is God's will for me? What will God have me do in this situation? Am I making this decision based on my feelings or emotions? Are my allowing my thoughts to wonder off and seek to get things done my way? Could this be a test of my faith in God?

_____

_____

_____

_____

_____

_____

These questions should lead you back to God so that you can begin to learn at His feet and view life from His perspective. This is how you begin to establish the foundation and understanding of unconditional love. You begin to learn how to be patient while waiting to hear from God. You realize that there is no life without Him and everything outside of His will for you is vanity, wasted time and energy that will only lead you to become frustrated, tired or repeat patterns.

You have to learn to set boundaries so that you do not compromise who you are with the standard of the world, culture or tradition. You have to learn to stand in your own truth. You have to be able to recognize a test of your faith and know how to overcome obstacles while turning them into stepping stones. Daniel did that. He stood his ground and stood in his truth. He refused to compromise his faith in God and ended up in the lion's den. Joseph stood too and refused to compromise his body with Potiphar's wife. He knew his purpose and did not want to fall off the wagon. His faith was tested when he was thrown in jail but he patiently waited while learning the lessons of not trusting man but God. He did fulfill his purpose.

The changes you need to make while single can only be done without distractions, recognition of your body as God's temple, patiently learning to love yourself and discover your purpose while building an intimate relationship with God. You cannot afford to compromise who you are and hop into every relationship.

You have to find your partner as God deemed. The rib or the one missing a rib. You cannot rush the process of change. You have to allow God prepare you through your journey and you have to become complete before finding a wife and allowing a husband to find you. The process is about learning on becoming the you God created not the one you envisage or are planning to make. The process is part of your growth and shift towards a higher self.

As couples, you will need to learn about and understand each other. You have to also understand that marriage is a representation of God's Kingdom on earth. The husband, wife and children represent The Trinity – God the Father, God the Son and God the Holy Spirit. For this reason, the husband must love his wife as Christ loved the church (Ephesians 5: 22-26). You cannot change your husband or wife. You have to pray and allow God do the work of change. You have to let go of ego so that you can learn while humble. Learning will not take place if you are selfish...that is not an attribute of love. You have to immerse yourself in love so that you can truly love your husband or wife.

As a single person, loving yourself will create you for you to love someone else. You have to understand that true love does not depend on conditions becoming favorable or not. It speaks in truth and with correction. Love strengthens not weakens. Love does not operate in seasons. It cannot be measured but will treasure you.

The more you see yourself through God's eyes, the easier it becomes to see other's through the same lenses. The more you love yourself, the easier it will be to give and share love with others. The more you learn, the more you grow and the more you change your thoughts, change your ways and change the world!

NUGGET 10

Living Truthfully
and Purposefully

So far you have grasped the knowledge about loving your-self, the consequences that come with disobedience and the importance of learning the lessons. You need to know that going forward you cannot bring the old lifestyle with you if you want to keep heading in the right and positive direction while living in love and truthfully.

You cannot put new wine in the old wineskin (Mark 2: 22). You have healed, learned to forgive and you are now ready and committed to live truthfully and purposefully. You are about to get out of the wilderness and dungeon of bad relationships to build on healthier and long-lasting ones.

RECOGNIZING DISTRACTIONS

As you begin the journey to living truthfully and purposefully, you have to be able to identify distractions as they come along to derail you from the course of your journey of life and love. Distractions always look like the real deal but they are not. The purpose of distractions is to ensure you do not continue to live the life of abundance God created for you. Distractions often cause chaos and drama especially when you are feeling lonely or bored. It is easy to become distracted when your mind, spirit and soul are not in sync. Distractions will raise your emotions and make you feel high and on the fly. They come filled with lies, packaging and shades only to leave you at the end in pain and shame. Distractions show up when you are looking for a short cut to success or a quicker way of being in a relationship and forge ahead. The sugarcoated lies meet you at your comfort zone so you quickly agree to settle for those and give in, thus, you are left hurt or broken.

Reality is that love is free but you can only truly experience it when you have healed from the painful past and any form of brokenness. This is when you begin to easily recognize distractions because you are no longer looking for someone to soothe your pain but to tell you the truth in love...no packaging, no shades, no gimmicks and no antics.

Once you have fully healed, you will not go back to repeating patterns.

Joseph was able to recognize Potiphar's wife as a distraction to his journey of purpose. Jesus was able to recognize the devil as a distraction to his calling. Temptations are distractions and can come in any form or way. As a single person, distractions come in form of lust and imitated partners. They display their antics and make you defile your temple (body). You may think you have found the one but may have found the deceiver.

It may look like the real deal but will only fizzy out after a few days, months or weeks. You will sometimes have distractions come your way to test your faith and stand, to awaken you to becoming conscious of what aspect is lacking and has a need to be met...a level of you wanting to grow deeper. Not everyone you meet is a potential partner and not every relationship will end up to be romantic. Some will test your faith and walk with God while others will teach you a lesson or two that leads to your growth. Remember, you have a choice to give in or to stand out and say no to distractions. *"God is faithful; He will not let you be tempted beyond what you can bear" – 1 Corinthians 10: 13*. For you to learn how to avoid distractions, you need to be able to understand the difference between wants and needs.

VIEW DISAPPOINTMENTS AS LIFE'S TEACHER

No one wants to be disappointed by others. We always have the desire that everything will work for our good but that is not always the case. We set expectations that may be too high or low and end up getting disappointment.

The truth is that as long as there is something for us to learn in life, we will continue to get hurt and be disappointed.

Disappointments are blessings in disguise, if only we take time to think through and see how they serve as life's teacher.

Facing disappointments leaves us hurt and sometimes broken but if we shift our mindset and allow ourselves to view them as a source of growth (through pain), we will come to embrace them as stepping stones to learning a lot about ourselves and they may serve as a source for us to achieve great things in life.

> *Ask yourself every time you are faced with a disappointment, "What is there for me to learn?" "How can this result in my growth?"*

Give yourself a moment or two to process those thoughts. Write down anything that came up for you as you asked those questions. Do you observe anything different? Where there really lessons learned from each disappointment? I have had to do this exercise myself and this has resulted in a shift in mindset for me and I have come to realize that there are more things I can learn when I see disappointments as opportunities to grow and learn something new.

Think about it this way:
The storm you face is your teacher.
The experience you gain is your lesson.
The life you make out of it all is your blessing.
Always remember, that the teacher teaches a lesson that becomes a blessing.

Embrace each storm and watch your life change as you utilize the lessons.
Your better days lie ahead of you. Just hold on!"

– Kemi Sogunle

Each disappointment can be a storm but we must allow it teach us the lesson(s), so that we can gain the experience(s) from the lesson(s) learned. This will in turn result in a blessing as we gain knowledge to become wiser, stronger and a better version of us that God created. Life is after all about learning and growing. We do not stop learning until our time here on earth expires. Embrace each disappointment and let it serve as life's best teacher. People may walk out of your life. Some will let you down. The truth is: you can't own anyone. You can't lose anyone that was meant to be in your life forever. You have to realize that when someone's season is over, there is nothing you can do to keep them in your life. It may hurt for a while but the lessons you learned will serve you for a lifetime!

PONDER ON THIS:

What have you learned about disappointments? How are you going to allow each one you have experienced teach you life's lessons? How are you planning to turn them into your own blessings?

_____

_____

_____

Understanding Needs versus Wants

You have both wants and needs but it is important that you recognize they are not the same. Wants only serve temporary purposes while needs exist for long term reasons. Everything you need to survive on earth was provided by God when you were created. However, you have to tap into your spirituality and speak life into yourself while using your skills. You also have to be patient while having hope (both are attributes of love). Knowing what you need, varies with your growth and the stage you are in life. For example, you may need a job and your skills will be what you require to be able to meet that need while finding a job. Without those skills, you may settle for another job because you think it is a want. The same happens in a relationship. You need a partner that will complement you but you settle for a partner who does not, because you are lonely.

Your needs should be in line with the tangibles that will help you continue to grow and move forward in your journey...your values, your goals and aspirations or your requirements for finding a partner – compatibility, chemistry and commitment.

Set goals to accomplish your goals and meet your needs. Take care of yourself...spirit, soul, mind and body. If there is a disconnection between your spirit, mind and body, you will have a longing for something within you to reconnect the three.

CHALLENGE

What are some of your needs that you need to identify? What do you need to do to challenge yourself to meet those needs?

_____

_____

_____

_____

_____

_____

How do you plan to handle distractions when you come across them?

_____

_____

_____

_____

_____

_____

TAKING CARE OF YOU AND YOUR BODY

You have to take care of you and your body before you can take care of anyone else. It is extremely important for you to know and understand that you are created complete and the longing or yearning to be with someone, is usually the search for what is missing in your life that will lead to you feeling and realizing you are complete. Know that your body is the

temple of God (1 Corinthians 6:19-20) and the Spirit of God
resides in you. If you are disconnected from the Spirit of God
living in you, you will have that longing and yearning feeling
to find what is missing. The Holy Spirit allows you to connect back with God and feel whatever empty void that may
exist. This is why you have to continue to build on the solid
foundation and relationship with God.

Think about it as building a house. You have to lay the solid foundation for which you will build on. The foundation
has to be strong enough to hold the pieces together. Without
the solid foundation and established relationship with God
which results in a peaceful life, chaos is all you will receive.
You will become distracted, give in to temptation and lose
yourself in the process. The process is not mean to derail you
but to shape you into who God created you to be. The process will refine and redirect you in the path God laid when
you were created.

You have to learn to master your own body and control
your soul and mind in alignment with God's will. This is often hard to do when you allow your emotions to run the race
in your mind but the moment you start to align your
thoughts with God's thoughts, it becomes really doable.

One of the reasons why we often allow the physical side of
us to overshadow the spiritual side, is that we focus on what
is seen than the unseen and we allow our emotions that have
been given to us to lead and guide us back to God, act as the
principal source that leads us astray. The more we focus on
what is seen than the unseen, the less faith and hope we have
and the less we think that we need God in our lives. You must
learn to tame your thoughts, control your mind and allow the

Spirit of God to take care of you when you become emotional than let your thoughts tame you, awaken fear and ego and cause you to go off track.

> *What you allow to rule and reign in you, your body, mind and soul, will dominate your life.*

You have to learn to awaken your faith so that you can be more hopeful. You have to continue to learn to love yourself on a daily basis in order for you to become kinder to yourself, patient with yourself, speak the truth to yourself, honor yourself, respect yourself, keep no record of the past and do to yourself as you would have others do to you (and vice versa). Without loving yourself, no one can love you like you would. Celebrate your little wins, be grateful for your journey and growth. Own your moments and truth and do not compromise who you are for little pleasures that will lead to consequences of pain. Focus on building your relationship with God so that you can really know and understand who you are and whose you are.

You also have to take care of your body, mind and soul by forgiving yourself. Allowing yourself to become free of all the stress and tension you have placed on your body and mind that may have shifted you from the course of your journey or resulted in you having health issues. Allowing worries, hurt, pain, bitterness or resentment rule and reign over your body and mind will put a negative effect and take a significant toll on your health. Aligning your mind with the ways and plans of God will however, help you stay on track with your life's purpose (with the help of the Holy Spirit.

How has holding on the painful past experiences affected your mind, soul and body? What changes do you need to make going forward?

_____

_____

_____

_____

_____

THE PURPOSEFUL RELATIONSHIP

As a single person, those sexual feelings will come as a distraction but you have to realize that finding the partner God created for you, is better than settling for just anyone who comes across your way. The need is to meet the partner, the want is to settle for sex or lust. The want is temporary and the need is long term. The thoughts will come but you have to learn to tame your thoughts and not allow your thoughts tame you. Start with you and focus on doing the following:

1. **Focus on Building a Solid Relationship with God**
    As a single person, allow your relationship with God grow deeper and let it be the foundation for which you build your relationship on with your partner.

    As married couples, establish the foundation with God so that your relationship can grow and glow in the purpose for which He brought you together. *"Seek first the Kingdom of God and His righteousness and all these things will be added unto you"* – Matthew 6: 33.

2. **Focus on Discovering Yourself and Your Purpose**
    You are created by God for a specific purpose (Jeremiah 29: 11). No one else can fulfill that purpose but you. Knowing who you are and your purpose in life will set the pace for finding a partner and allowing your partner find you.

3. **Focus on Guarding your Purity**
    We live in a sexually saturated world and to keep yourself pure, can be challenging. However, it is easy to do when you choose to become determined to know and value yourself. Remember that you are God's temple and if you purpose in your heart to value His temple and not disrespect it with a few minutes of lustful pleasure, your partner will respect you for that.

    God took a rib out of one man to make that one woman for him and from him. He had a purpose for their relationship. He placed them in the garden to fulfill that purpose. They both recognized each other when they met...no infatuation or lust involved. They knew who they were. God created both male and female in His Image and Likeness...pure, sanctified and a holy temple. God created the woman and brought her of his side, to be his helpmate. As a woman, when you give in to a relationship outside of what God has defined it to be, you are saying, "God I do not respect You or myself but choose to defy this temple and disconnect from You."

You have to flee from immorality, knowing that your body belongs to God and His Spirit dwells in you to bring Him glory.

4. **Focus on Developing God Character and Qualities**
You do not shop for shoes or clothes without trying them to see if they will fit. You would not buy anything that is smaller or bigger than the size you wear. The same applies when it comes to building your character in a godly manner. You do not want to have attributes that would not match up with that of God. Always remember that you are created in God's image and after His likeness.

To be a reflection of our Heavenly Father requires that we develop qualities that allow others to see Him in our daily living. You and I are created as the salt of the earth and the light of the world (Matthew 5: 13-16). A godly partner should be able to see these qualities in you and they should also be a reflection of who he or she is. This will allow you build on a relationship that will honor God.

It is important that you note that having a relationship will not solve the problem of loneliness while single but it will help you develop and build on your relationship with God. Loneliness should lead you to soul searching and finding yourself. The empty feeling that comes with loneliness is a longing to connect to your true essence and to God so that you can better understand your purpose and begin to love and see yourself in that light. The moment you are fully healed and are connected to God spiritually, no one will have the power to break or hurt you.

You are now walking in your truth and light. You are able to recognize distractions when they come knocking. You can pick the red flags quickly during the initial conversation. It is very important that you focus on building purposeful and truthful relationships that will help you stay on track with your purpose and vision for your life. You also will add value to those who you build this relationship with while they do the same in your life.

5. **Know That You Are Good Enough**

You sometimes may think you are not good enough. You may use words negative or derogatory words to describe yourself when you fail at one thing. However, labelling yourself will only reinforce pain or show your lack for self-confidence. This can alter your belief system and make negative thinking become your reality. God created you and saw you were God. He released you from the spiritual realm into the physical realm as good enough.

Purposeful Relationships are not based on your weaknesses but see beyond that into the heart and the connection is spiritually based than physically attached. There is an awakening in your spirit to recognize the partner or person you are with knows who they are in Christ and God and will not see you outside of that realm. He or she recognizes your purpose and life's mission and will complement you in that aspect.

How Purposeful is your relationship with your partner, friends or family members?

_____

_____

_____

_____

_____

_____

PONDER ON THIS:

What label are you placing on yourself that is limiting you or making you remain stuck without seeing your value or worth?

_____

_____

_____

_____

_____

_____

The woman who was labeled the 'adulterous woman' when brought to Jesus by her accusing was found to have no label neither was she condemned. Jesus asked her accuser to cast the first stone if they had no sin but none of them could. He told her to go and sin no more. (1 John 8: 1-11).

How hard do you hold on the painful experiences from the past or allow the memories to linger and hold you a prisoner of your thoughts?

_____

_____

_____

_____

_____

_____

You must realize that the things you hold on to, are only going to hold you a prisoner of your own thoughts and mind. God knows you by name and knows everything you will venture into outside of His will for your life. He awaits you to come back to Him for forgiveness of anything outside His will for you. He does not see you as you see yourself. What others think does not determine who God says you are. They did not create you or write your story. You have to keep your focus on God and your journey while seeking His face for help throughout life. The crowd condemned the woman but God granted her mercy.

This is the same way He grants you and I mercy and still brings us to see a brand new day every morning. He sets the pace and course for your life not man or woman. He still sees that you are worthy of turning to Him to live that life He created for you from the inception. What are you waiting for? What is stopping you? What is clouding your vision of who you are? What are you going to do today to change that?

_____

_____

_____

_____

I want you to realize that no matter what you are facing or have gone through, nothing or no one defines you but God. Weeping may endure for the night but your joy will surely come in the morning. You only suffered because you did not understand who God says you are but now that you are becoming aware of who you truly are, know that you are indeed a miracle. You are 'perfectly imperfect.' No one can be you. You are uniquely created and shaped by The Master and you are indeed GOOD ENOUGH!

6. **Do Not Lie to Yourself**

   There are times when you will feel lonely and someone shows up with seductions to derail you and lead you to compromise who you are for what you want or crave for in that moment. You may observe the red flags and part of you (your flesh) will want you to ignore those. You may lie to yourself while they are also lying to you to win you over and choose to settle.

   However, choosing to settle and give in, will only lead to regrets later on as well as the consequences you will have to face. You ought to know that the partner God created for you, will never have to lie to you or expect you to give in and get hurt. If his or her vision is not aligned with yours, there is no need for you to give in and get hurt. The same applies to friendships.

Are your friends aligned with your purpose or vision? Are they there to test you? Are they there to distract you? What have you noticed about your friends regarding your vision and purpose in life?

_____

_____

_____

_____

_____

_____

What lies are you telling yourself to keep them around? Are they there to massage your ego or to tell you the truth even when it hurts?

_____

_____

_____

_____

_____

_____

Relationships have to occur in life but there are those who will break, shape and mold or push you to find who you are and everything relationship has a season and a reason. You have to make the necessary adjustments in life...packing up comfort, unpacking to compromise or refusing to pack what you do not need in your space and life. You have to be able to control your emotions and not allow your emotions control you during this process in your journey.

Finding a partner requires that you evaluate where you are, know what you need and require and leave alone what you do not need. If it like moving from one house to another (you moving to a higher level of self). You do not take with you all the items in the house. You sort through and filter out giveaways, trash and things you plan to move. You cannot rush the process if you plan to get rid of things you do not need. You cannot say yes to everyone you meet without evaluating him or her to see if they are in sync with your vision and purpose. You will need quality time to build the friendship, trust, know and understand each other before you both can decide what the next step is for you and your relationship.

Always remember that there is a time and season for everything (Ecclesiastes 3). Rushing before time will result in pain or consequences that will not yield positive results. Learning to wait shows the attribute of love – patience, in you. For the married, remember that marriage is a sacred union created to honor God not man. "Husbands are to love their wives as Christ loved the church and gave Himself up for her...to make her holy, cleansing her by the washing with water through the word and to present her to Himself as a radiant church without stain or wrinkle or any blemish but holy and blameless. Ephesians 5: 25-27." Your role as a husband is to be a covering for your wife. Washing her with the word of God so that she can be grounded in her faith and walk with Him. You do not create room for her to do the blaming. You create room for her to become blameless.

However, without you loving God and knowing who you are in Him, this will be very difficult to accomplish. You have to have a vision and purpose for your life and that will set the pace for the woman you are looking to make your wife. Her vision and purpose should be aligned with yours. Without knowing your purpose and hers as well as the vision, it will be hard to create one for your marriage and know the direction in which to go.

As a husband, you have to rejoice in the wife of your youth (Proverbs 5:18-19) and this does not have anything to do with age. Age is just a number. You have to embrace and saturate her with your love. You both grow and glow together in love.

As a wife, you are created to be your husband's helpmate. To support and cheer him on. You have to be submissive by allowing him play the role God created him for. He will bring to the table a discussion and you support him with the plan. You set time aside to build into one another, study the word, pray and communicate effectively. You have to keep your marriage bed undefiled by avoiding distractions that will lead you into adultery. You have to ensure you have each other's back. You do not stop courting your wife but you create your relationship

C.L.O.U.D.

C – create an atmosphere of love that will help you build into one another as well as your relationship daily.

L – leave past issues behind and do not bring them up to cause disruptions, distractions or chaos.

O – open up to one another and be willing to support each other without being judgmental or prejudice.

U – uphold one another in everything and in every possible way. This will strengthen your relationship.

D – develop an attitude of gratitude especially for those little things you ignore.

Devote time to pray with and for one another. Spend time together in God's presence as a couple. Remember, the head cannot function without the neck. The same applies to your marriage. You both need each other to grow. Allow God to be the center of your relationship without pushing Him to the curb. He will uphold your union and it will last a lifetime.

What will you do going forward to build on healthier relationships with your partner?

_____

_____

_____

_____

_____

_____

Bottom Line

The Prodigal Journey – Luke 15: 11-32

The Prodigal son ventured of his father's estate. He wanted to live a life of his own. He took his inheritance and sailed off to party and lavish his wealth. He spent everything in no time and began working to make ends meet. He could not keep up with his lifestyle any longer. He went from one job to another and ended up feeding pigs. He ate from the pig's stall. Can you imagine going from being the wealthy child to become poor? However, he came to his senses and realized that his father has the best of the best. He was going to go back and try work for his father so that he can stop existing and begin to live. He recalled how his father treated the servants.

It was better than his current situation. He had made poor choices and now needed to make restitution and return to love.

His father was the loving man who will not turn him down but open his arms wide to welcome him back. That is exactly what God did, receive the Prodigal Son back. He was thrown a party and a signet ring was placed on his finger with the best robes on his back.

Where are you in your journey? What do you need to do to return to God...Love Himself? Do you know He will not judge not condemn you when you return but welcome you home and celebrate you? What is stopping you from returning to Love...God?

_____

_____

_____

_____

_____

_____

THE TRUTH

The journey of life and love is not going to be an easy one. We must learn how to walk in between the thorns of life while seeing obstacles as our stepping stones to greatness. To fully understand what love is, you have to build on a solid foundation of an intimate relationship with God while allowing Him to fully lead and guide you in the way of love. You must learn to love yourself completely until you become complete and whole. Loving yourself not only creates the awareness of your needs, requirements and purpose but allows you to set boundaries, focus on accomplishing your purpose and allow love find and complement you.

Roses have thorns but it is how you find your way around the thorns that maters in life.

You have to see beyond the pain or struggle and learn to live life to the fullest. Hold your head up high and make every moment count while you still have the chance. Always remember that life is a gift from God. You must live, love, laugh and learn. No one can walk or work your journey. However, you have to build on your relationships in the right order...God first, then you before others. You have to stop repeating patterns by taking things into your own hands without seeking God for direction and guidance. You have to break the cycle of generation curses.

You have to untie your soul and most importantly, you have to find and love yourself. The truth is that the word hate was used to describe the situation for which the world will have to hate you when you are following God and walking with Him. The truth is that until you are ready to won your truth, you will keep living in your shadow and throwing shades. The truth is that we all were born in love but the world tries to take that part of us away so we do not know who we are.

The truth is that no man can take God's glory when He restores you and gives you a brand new start. The truth is God is ready to change your story but you have to be determined to want to change. The truth is that your flesh will die someday but your spirit will return to God and the time you have is only known to The Maker.

No matter what color, race or gender, the same blood continues to flow through each one of us...the blood which is a sign of God's love and part of His Master Plan. We cannot continue to tear each other apart with hurt. We must all heal, move beyond the pain and return to love. It must begin with each person, each household and each community. Everything else will cease but love will always remain.

> *The color of love will never change. The color of love cannot die in vain.*

Love is all we need to keep us going and growing. Love is who we are. You have to live in your truth so that you can fully and truly appreciate the love that you are. God continuously reminds you and I through the life, breath, air and grace He grants us each brand new day. This is the time to fully embrace God's love. The time is now to Return to Love and live again.

Always remember that love is bigger than life. If you do not fully love yourself, you cannot truly live the life God created for you. Without love there will be no life and you will not have the opportunity to give or share love with others. Let love be your light and let your light shine for others to see. There is no life outside of God.

"Love the Lord with all your heart, all your soul, all your strength and all your mind. Love your neighbor as yourself" – Luke *10: 27. "Whoever claims to love God, yet hates a brother or sister is a liar. For whoever does not love their brother or sister, whom they have seen, cannot love God whom they have not seen"* – John *4: 20.*

Everything points us back to Him. Learn to move beyond the pain, experience the love of God, learn to love yourself so that you can love others and allow love to find you. Learn to build your home in love and with love. You cannot say you do not need anyone or want to stand alone. You need God, you need to connect with yourself and build relationships with others. You need to find your missing rib and your rib to be able to complement one another. You cannot walk this road alone without having love or experiencing love through your journey. This is the reason why you have to choose to move beyond the pain and return to love so that you can experience life again as God planned it. Choose life, choose love and choose to live...with love you can conquer!

Everything we do involves relationships...beginning with a relationship with God and allowing the Holy Spirit to teach us those things we need to know. We come in contact with others during our journeys of purpose and our weaknesses show up and bring about conflicts when we allow ego and fear to dominate rather than allow the Holy Spirit to humble us to see beyond the pain. We must learn to show love and give the love that we are to others without judgement. There is no judgement in love...only correction. We must learn to let go of yesterday and see the beauty of today. Bringing along yesterday only creates room to live in the past and it takes away God's Divine Plan for today. This will only create chaos for tomorrow and oozes in with lingering pain and hurt. That is why Christ laid it down by saying in Matthew 6: 34," Therefore *do not worry about tomorrow, for tomorrow will worry about itself. Each day has enough trouble of its own.*" You can only live in the present moment. That is all that is with God.

Living in the present moment creates the atmosphere for love and life without hurt or pain. You are not caged in the past or forging ahead because you know all you have in now...this moment! You are able to create room for happiness and pray for happiness for those who hurt or offended you. You have come to realize that the pain is not about you but where they are and showing them love is part of your commitment and purpose. This is what love is all about.

I have learned through this journey that there is no greater way but love. Without love we are nothing. God is love and we are His children...born of love and not hurt. The world teaches us otherwise. The culture and tradition derail and deny us of the truth. The same way the serpent deceived Eve, many are being deceived today...completely brainwashed from perceiving and living their realties. I have chosen to continue to coach, speak and write as a way of supporting others through this journey called life. It is short, live it in truth and in love. You never know when God will call you back but you do not want to live without love and love without living. Choose to return to love and never stop loving while living...when you stop loving, you stop living!

About the Author

Kemi Sogunle is a **multi-award-winning author, international speaker, fashion/image consultant and certified professional coach** (listed as one of the best 10 coaches in Maryland, USA by Thumbtack.com and featured as a contributor to The Huffington Post, a Dating Expert on Older Dating UK, Inspirations and Celebrations) and Fashion Contributor/Image Consultant in the BWI Magazine. She has also been featured in Essence and Bustle. Kemi is the **Founder/CEO** of the **nonprofit** organization (501c3), Love Not Hurt, an organization that promotes self-development, building healthier and stronger relationships while living with purpose.

Mission: Kemi's **mission/purpose** in life is to **support single men and women who are ready, to find who they are** after a broken relationship or divorce, **heal from their painful past experiences, learn to love themselves** and develop **positive and healthier relationship habits.** You will learn how to gain a deeper understanding of your life and relationship vision while living **truthfully and purposefully** to make your life become **better not bitter.**

Her Story: She writes and speaks from a personal place and **experience on relationships, healing, forgiveness and pur-**

poseful living by **moving from pain to purpose**. Kemi began her journey to becoming a life and relationship coach after her separation and divorce, which led her to soul-searching. Raped at age 17, she kept this to herself and never healed from it. This led her to looking for love in the wrong places. After her painful divorce, she embarked on a journey to finding herself and she connected to her spirituality while learning to viewing life from a different perspective. She found herself, healed and gained a deep understanding of life and relationships as well as her purpose in life. She shares deep and inspirational messages through her writing and has touched many lives across the globe. She also teaches and inspires others to become the best version of the person God created them to be on daily basis. She believes that **living truthfully is paramount to long-lasting relationships and healthy living**.

Connect with Kemi

Books Published
- Love, Sex, Lies and Reality
- Being Single: A State for the Fragile Heart
- Beyond the Pain: A Return to Love

Social Media
- Facebook: www.facebook.com/lovesexliesandreality
- Twitter: @kemisogunle
- Instagram: @kemisogunle
- Website: www.kemisogunle.com
- Email: coaching@kemisogunle.com
- YouTube: www.youtube.com/c/kemisogunle

For Speaking Engagements, email:
booking@kemisogunle.com

For Life and Relationship Coaching, email:
coaching@kemisogunle.com

For Online Courses on Life and Relationships:
http://bit.ly/2cY4nMO

www.ingramcontent.com/pod-product-compliance
Lightning Source LLC
Chambersburg PA
CBHW071439090426
42737CB00011B/1711